Twi

An Explo
the U

by Ronald Kinsella

To Brenda with love Ronni xx

www.capallbann.co.uk

Twin Souls

Cover design by HR Print and Design Ltd
Illustrations by Ronald Kinsella

Published by:

Capall Bann Publishing
Auton Farm
Milverton
Somerset
TA4 1NE

Dedication

I dedicate this book to the TV and Radio presenter, Paul Salmon, a gentleman who has inspired me no end, and has helped me throughout the course of my own literary progress, along with the author, John West. Both these kind souls have dedicated their lives to seeking answers relating to the supernatural and their integrity is unmatched.

It is also for Sue Barker for her kindness and support of all my work.

For the author, Annie Frame. Annie has given me an unimaginable boost regarding my work and I am indebted to this kind Angel for her belief in me.

For my publishers, Jon and Julia Day, whom I am extremely grateful to and who do not frown upon a testimony that stretches beyond that of the norm.

Finally, for my brother, Philip - my true and purest soul mate - who has travelled with me throughout the course of aged empires and lands of dust and gold. My mirror - my reflection of truth...

Endorsement from Brenda Butler, co-author of 'Sky Crash'

'*Twin Souls*' is a book that will offer you hope. Having read it, I was left feeling intrigued by the events that occurred during Ronald's experiences, though not surprised. Having researched the UFO subject for decades, I am utterly convinced that mankind, as a whole, is - and has been - visited by advanced beings from other worlds and dimensions, and that civilisation must look upon this phenomena as a reality; rather that a laughable dinnertable topic.

'*Twin Souls*' begins with a startling encounter concerning, what I believe to be, a classic 'Grey Alien' and weaves a web of fascinating incidents regarding not only that of the extra-terrestrials, but also the Spiritual Dimension. Ronald's honesty is both warm and charming and I can say, with hand-on-heart, that his book will help and inspire many people.

Make of it what-you-will, but remember (and if you are new to the subject of UFO's and Spiritual contact) - and as Ronald rightly demonstrates - be mindful in your approach to this subject. For him, his very own dismissal ironically led to a series of events that shattered his ignorance and of which led him to finally believe that we, as a species, are not alone.

Brenda Butler

Contents

Titles by Philip Kinsella, published by Capall Bann:

Reaching For the Divine - How To Communicate
Effectively With Your Spirit Guides & Loved Ones On The
Other Side

Believe - A Ground-Breaking Theory Which Bridges the
Gap Between the Psychic and UFO Phenomena

"I was a non-believer, but that has now changed. My own arrogance and narrow-minded views have been shattered by astonishing supernatural incidents, and I am prepared for scorn and ridicule from those who cannot conform to such possibilities. I am not here to preach or to alter views. Indeed, if people prefer to turn a blind eye from such radical notions, then so-be-it. I have no ego to bruise and most certainly do not wish to be at loggerheads with those willing to tear my testimony to shreds."

Ronald Kinsella is the twin brother of the author and award-winning Medium, Philip Kinsella. In this book, he highlights incidents that changed his perception of life. From extra-terrestrial encounters to conversations with Spirit, this account spans his struggle in coming to terms with alter-native worlds and dimensions.

Chapter One

The Thing in the Garden

As children, I found that people tended to fuss over Philip and myself due to the fact that back then (in 1969) identical twins were something of a novelty. Nowadays, they are respectfully more common than ever and, when we were growing up, triplets became the next best thing for the tabloids to gloat over. Consequently, even this phenomenon outgrew its own charm.

I lived with a family who had moved homes more than not, and who also planned to immigrate to South Africa, which transpired in 1975; the change of which was brief due to personal reasons. My brother and I were happy (along with our sister Chris who was born in 1974) and so, as children, the very notion of other worldly experiences was far removed from our adolescent lives - as you would certainly come to expect from kids - had it not been for the fact that I saw an extra-terrestrial when I was just four years old.

This extra-terrestrial is what ufologists would commonly deem as being a classic Grey; though it was not grey in colour at all, but whitish-beige and the memory of it did not surface until I was in my mid twenties. Water of all things evoked this most bizarre incident and I shall shortly describe to you how it happened. The recollection of the encounter is as fresh today as it was when I first recalled it ... and one which haunts me.

On a note regarding identical siblings, I heard somewhere - I think on a TV channel exploring the validity of UFO encounters - that aliens (or whatever they are) theoretically display more of a keen interest in twins. Whether this is true or not, I have no idea, though I have often wondered if a biological counterpart appeals to them, due to their supposed (and of what I have read in many books) cloning programme.

I cannot question the validity of this because I simply have no answers at this time, though I have an idea, and one which I shall express. Even so, what remains real and absolute is that I have seen one of these things up close, and it was a harrowing experience.

*   *   *

Philip and I were born in Oxfordshire on April 12th 1969 and, from an early age, were close. Even today, we are very much inseparable and our relationship has generated both interest and scorn from people of all walks of life. Interest for the best part, with the scorn emerging from those who deem adult males living together as both weird and unacceptable, and whose psychological morals based on this outlook - as intelligent as they are - puzzles me. To my mind, they embrace an unbending sense of arrogance if they snigger or offer harsh opinions, when clearly they fail to understand the reason for twins liking their own company, rather than others. I sometimes wonder how they can possibly open their eyes to supernatural occurrences, such as what I have documented, if they adopt stagnant views that men living together are abnormal.

This book is not about intrigue or a selfish way of exploiting an alien encounter, along with spiritual matters and coincidences that cannot possibly be coincidences. No, this is about the power of the unknown and how it subtly found its way into both Philip's and my life. I hope, with hand on heart, that it may inspire people to look at themselves and to re-evaluate, if necessary, their way of thinking once they have read about the trials we both faced, along with the wonderment of the unexplained.

Indeed, being a twin has helped to shape my life. And, having been introduced to the supernatural - through the bonus of having a psychic brother - I have embraced it with an open mind; knowing that there is more to this curious enigma than meets the eye. It also unleashed my dogmatic views in a world where the impossible became the possible; with belief shaping reality. And, once I trusted in the people of 'Heaven', they helped me overcome many hurdles with astonishing results.

So now we begin the story of my first encounter and, subsequently, my memory of it unwittingly being erased, only to find myself ridiculing the entire UFO/ Spiritual enigma; until I recalled the incident, along with discovering a dimension almost parallel to our own and which we have come to know as 'Heaven.'

The stagnant age-old view that, "It is so much easier for people to accept your testimony when, at first, you disbelieve it yourself" is pure nonsense and immediately places a negative outlook on documentations relating to the supernatural. I have heard some hogwash in my time, I can tell you, with people preferring to use the most ridiculous anecdotes to cover incredible encounters and experiences that effect others on a daily basis all over the world. They do this not because they are ignorant, I believe, but because they are terrified, being that it does not conform to their comfortable, school-indoctrinated, TV drama induced, family-complying and normal-behavioural world.

I hope you will understand the truth of my words as I am not afraid to join - what others might deem - crackpots or sensationalists ... or other brutal words conjured to put the likes of us in a pigeon hole conveniently labelled 'X-File Nut.'
It also staggers me to realise that, when sound-minded people relay their supernatural experiences on numerous chat-shows broadcast on TV or Cable, a so-called expert is more-than-not

on hand to offer a rational, if not, downright ludicrous explanation. I liken the interviewee as being an inferno - the raging flames of their experiences either representing hope or fear - with the so-called specialist symbolising a bucket of water, preparing to douse out the flames to the relief of the masses; thus extinguishing any threat and restoring security and order to the public.

After all, they can all sleep sound in their beds, knowing that tales of such encounters are as outlandish as the very idea of people surviving death.

*   *   *

Children from birth and up to the age of 6 cannot, I believe, imagine; not in the way we can. Having been children ourselves, I am sure you will agree that you cannot ever recall mentally envisioning a beautiful castle in your mind, or that of a world, perhaps, better than this one, up to the age I have specified. Indeed, it is quite safe to assume that the mind of the infant is still in its early stages of development; concentrating on understanding its surroundings, noises, vision and the arduous task of language, among many other things the brain is required to adopt.

Toys are important to children because they offer interaction; helping to develop the necessary skills they need to improve, such as touch, sight, sound and balance and - once these have been achieved - they move on to more complex tools to help aid their ways in an ever demanding world that is invariably waiting for them.

Ah, but what of the common imaginary friends they interact with and which are so frequent throughout? I hear you say. Well, this leads to a more shocking revelation which I shall address later in the book and which cannot, under the basis of my logic, possibly be due to imagination; simply because the mind, at this stage, has not developed sufficiently enough to offer the inner-eye of conscious dreaming.

How can it?

This is leading to my experience with the extra-terrestrial I saw when I was four years old. And no, I am not trying to justify these facts simply to make the encounter fit. That, in itself, would be damaging. And, before we move on to the incredible incident, I could not - as with my brother - mentally conceive or conjure creative images in my head, when both Philip and I were, like the rest of us no doubt, so reliant on those toys that stimulated our senses in every respect.

* * *

In 1972, Mum and Dad, along with Philip and myself, lived on an estate belonging to a prominent and pioneering eye surgeon of the time, Dr Thomas Gregory. The main house, or mansion if you prefer, was breathtaking in itself, though we lived in a large cottage within the premises, which was originally used as the servant's quarters. The estate boasted a trout stream, a tennis court and extensive land along with an outdoor swimming pool which had, to our fond memories, a statue of a fox lying before it.

Bignell House, near Chesterton, Oxfordshire, was the lap of luxury for its wealthy owners; having an imposing winding driveway which led up to the main house bypassing fields on both sides and which stretched from a gatehouse. Mum worked inside the house for the owners while Dad was left to tend the extensive lawns. Philip and I, along with Dad, were not allowed inside the mansion. The cottage where we lived was enormous and I can distinctly remember, in winter, our parents having to light the large fires within most of the rooms, even the bedrooms upstairs!

It's funny what you recall, even at the age of four. We had a golden Labrador called Prince, who used to pinch our lollipops from us, along with making a disobedient addition to the dinner table; with us feeding him titbits beneath it. I even recall his gentle teeth and warm tongue as he happily relieved me of my unwanted sausages. He was a little crazy too, so Mum recalls, with him abandoning us for days; having disappeared into the woods and refusing to return. She even went out looking for him in the dead of night, worried that he had vanished for good. Nonetheless, he always returned. He also used to charge up the driveway on occasions, disconcertingly slamming himself into the rear bumpers of cars. Mum was convinced he needed glasses!

Our Grandparents, Kath and Reginald King, used to visit us there at times and both Philip and I were always excited to see them; being spoilt with presents and very happy in their company. The family used to watch us play outside on our Mars-Hoppers, small tricycles or pedal-cars and the infrequent passage of weather balloons, drifting over the estate, made the days welcoming and surreal.

Philip and I were dressed identically on a daily basis more-than-not, sometimes wearing our matching chequered red jackets, shirts and ties, while often other times simple t-shirts and trousers. As boys, we never fought over a thing, not even our toys. This, I believe, is a testament to the twin thing because, genetically, we were and are the same. There was no cause for competition either, simply because we loved each other and that was that.

I cannot recall what day it was exactly when the incident occurred - as you would not expect a child of four to do so - though I do know that it was around summer time and, apart from a few clouds drifting overhead, the weather was moderately pleasant. Also, it must have been the early afternoon, or thereabouts, because this is the distinct impression I got when the event was unmercifully thrust into my consciousness later in life. On that note; it's as if the imminent encounter was so terrifying that my brain either automatically shut itself down to swiftly disregard it, or was conveniently instructed to overlook it.

I was out playing with Philip within the cottage garden that was securely fenced in, with both our parents no doubt busy with their chores; Mum never far off to keep a vigilant eye on us. Prince was not around - this being a usual trait of his - and he may have been frolicking in the woods for all I knew; being the rebellious mutt that he was.

Standing beside a cluster of plants in the garden, I stretched over and plucked one up. At this time, I do recall Philip being somewhere near and behind me, either playing on his tricycle or pedal-car - I'm not exactly sure what toy he was on or in - but he was certainly close.

But what I am certain of is that this plant I now had in my grasp became an object of fascination as I began to meticulously tear open its stem; noticing the fine fibres encompassing the interior of it; appearing almost like a whitish polystyrene compound. And, as I examined it with avid interest, something happened; something extremely bizarre!

Something jumped out of it! I remembered thinking it to be some kind of bug though, whatever it was, it managed to leap at such a fantastic height. I immediately threw the plant down in surprise, noticing the thing having landed in the sward before me. As I looked about to see where it had settled, I needn't have bothered.

The bug, within the blink of an eye and to my immediate horror, had swiftly transformed itself from the miniscule thing it was, into a towering creature that resembled some type of insect. As I gazed back at it in newfound dread, I noticed huge slanting black eyes peering at me, which were shiny and as dark as coal. Its complexion was that of a whitish-beige and I could clearly discern its head, neck and body - though its arms and legs were not registered, as I was primarily transfixed by its peculiar and intent gaze.

It was around four and a half feet tall, from what I could tell.

It just stood there to begin with; staring back at me, and it was as unimaginable as it was horrifying. Those eyes just peered into mine and, as I gawked back at it in stunned silence I felt or somehow knew that it was about to move.

And I was right!

With disconcerting swiftness and a blurriness I could not fathom, it advanced towards me. It was then when I began to scream.

Chapter Two

Amnesia & Recollection

I turned to run and, upon doing so, Philip must have also seen the thing because he, like me, began to flee and scream. However, as with something so terrifying, you are - more than not - likely to turn and look back to gage the distance of your tormentor. This, as we know, is a natural compulsion for human beings under such drastic ordeals; the fear driving you headlong as well as making certain that you are outwitting your oppressor's speed and agility.

I turned to look, and was startled to see it blurring as it advanced, appearing behind me and to my left. The way it moved was shocking and, even though it did not need to worry about covering a fair distance pursuing a toddler, its motion was utterly alien. As it sped forth, I could also hear something peculiar and which I will never forget!

It made a sort of clicking noise - or buzzing - and it was so intense that I blindly raced towards the cottage; the sound being somewhat intimidating. Again, I saw it blurring as it swiftly overtook me and, with Philip speeding off in another direction, I knew within my heart that it wanted me for something or other.

And then, quite abruptly, everything changed!

I was no longer screaming and fleeing, and nor was Philip. In an instant, or so it seemed, we were both outside the cottage and near the front door, eating - of all things - an ice cream. It was still light and I do know, from a strong impression, that it was the same day; only the passage of time must have lapsed instantaneous from the terrifying encounter. I do recall Mum being outside with us, possibly working away at something or other, along with Prince, who was skulking around; ready to secure his jaws on our treats the moment she was out of eyeshot. There were no tears, no dread and certainly no intruder to be seen either.

We had no memory of what had transpired and it was as though the entire episode never occurred.

I shall skip forward in time a moment, to let you know of some unusual UFO's both Philip and I spotted, shortly before the memory of the extra-terrestrial surfaced. On this point, I can't help but wonder if the sightings were deliberately instigated to evoke the Bignell House incident and, if so, why? There is, I feel, a connection and one which grows stronger as we progress through the course of the book.

*   *   *

When I was in my mid twenties, Philip and I witnessed several spectacular UFO sightings over a village where we lived, near Bedford. The village I speak of was not heavily populated then and was surrounded by impressive country-side, with the community being small and pleasant. Buses followed a dodgy timetable and we had a small railway station a mile or so up the road, that looked as though it had been built in the Victorian era.

We lived in a cul-de-sac and our house was situated snugly in the corner of it; boasting ample rooms to enjoy along with a modest sized garden.

The first of these UFO's Philip and I saw was shaped rather like a silver tube, only it must have been huge; being that it was perhaps a mile and a half, possibly two, away from our location and around a hundred feet up in the air. From our vantage point and upon viewing it, I have calculated that it must easily have stretched nearly 200-300 feet in length. At the time, our study was upstairs and so it afforded us a perfect view of this strange new addition to the scenery. I cannot recall how we ever came to spot it in the first place; only it was as though we were strangely meant to.

We observed it hovering over a thicket, curiously swinging backwards and forwards, very steadily, like a pendulum on a clock. Upon viewing it I do remember agreeing with Philip how bizarre it was, due to its disturbing and repetitive motion. It was just so weird! It remained visible for around half an hour.

Philip and I possessed a modest telescope and so we hastily set it up within the study and concentrated on catching the object within the magnified lens. Because it was perpetually swinging, we had trouble aligning the telescope; though I managed to anticipate its seemingly unbroken sway and finally got a clear view of it.

What I saw was amazing!

It was not a plane, balloon, weather device or optical illusion from what I could tell and I studied it in great detail. It appeared to be solid, bearing no seams or protrusions and there were no strings attached either; ruling out the possibility of it being some kind of experimental kite. No, this thing was completely unnatural.

Since we are familiar with our own aircraft and technology, it begs the question as to why - had it been some type of experimental and super-secret aircraft constructed by a university (there was one close by) - they would fly it near a communal establishment? In any case, the process of it swinging effortlessly in the sky with absolutely no evidence of an engine, propeller or exhaust port - so common with our conventional flying machines - would undoubtedly make the university rich overnight, due to the fact that they had finally conquered anti-gravitational propulsion.

Though the object appeared dense and large, I got the distinct impression that it was as light as a feather. And, before you palm-it-off as a helium-filled balloon, designed for atmospheric-testing, then think again. There was no breeze at all and the motion of it was calculated and precise.

Of course, after it vanished from sight, we dismissed the incident because people would either simply fob it off as a misinterpretation of something natural, or that it was merely an optical illusion. With incidents like these, as you may well come to expect, the world does not take kindly to people spotting UFO's and, if they do, there would have to be a perfectly rational explanation for them.

The second incident concerning a UFO happened sometime after, and which was corroborated by a local newspaper article. Not having recorded the exact day, due to my personal lack of interest in UFO's at the time, I do recall, however, that it must have been a year or so after the silver tube sighting, and during the summer season.

I was restless in bed that night and the bedroom I occupied was upstairs and faced the cul-de-sac, with the drawn curtains being light; offering the comforting glow of a streetlamp outside. The time was around midnight or there after, as I was always a late sleeper.

I heard a sound from outside and it was electronic in nature; progressively getting louder. It was like a continuous 'whooshing' noise - or an irritated engine of some kind - and, as I sat up in bed, I realised that it must be over the house. The resonance of it, I have to point out, did not belong to any conventional aircraft I am aware of.

The noise intensified and I got out of bed and approached the curtains to investigate. Upon doing so, I was besieged by a fantastic blast of light that penetrated the room. The only way I can describe this is as though somebody was taking a photograph of me with the flash engaged. The sound became so menacing that it instilled in me a certain degree of fear as I boldly drew back the drapes to find that, within an instant, the thing (whatever it was) along with the accompanying sound, had gone. The scenery outside was inert, with no aerial vehicle to be seen whatsoever.

It is quite peculiar how I merely climbed back into bed after that, giving the incident little thought. Apart from discussing it with Philip in the morning, I would have forgotten it altogether; had it not been for an article published in the local newspaper and which we received that Sunday.

Apparently, residents in the village of Clapham, bordering Bedford, witnessed a peculiar looking object in the sky at the dead of night and during that week. Strange lights and sounds were reported to have accompanied it and it caused quite a ruckus in one of the houses on approach; triggering the doors within to swing in an almost satirical fashion, as well as lighting the entire residence up in a deluge of unearthly radiance.

I remembered feeling a cold shiver run up my spine upon reading it; refusing to comment any further for fear of ridicule.

And then, after that, came the recollection of the thing in the garden.

* * *

As well as having a bathroom upstairs, our house also accommodated a separate shower room downstairs, beside the spare room. This, at the time, was being renovated and so, one morning, I reluctantly decided to take a bath. On that note, I absolutely detest baths, preferring the simple and quick act of washing beneath a cascade of water.

So I ran a bath and got in it, washing my hair in the process. Not wishing to use the hose to rinse out the shampoo - because I always manage to carelessly scald myself when trying to regulate the temperature - I propped myself up on my knees and scooped the water over my head. Upon doing so, I accidentally snorted a good dose of it up my nose.

Within a flash, I saw the events concerning the extra-terrestrial in the Bignell House garden unfold before me. It was so bizarre and poignant that I reeled back, flabbergasted and startled at the clarity of the vision; knowing full well that, in some strange way, the small mishap had evoked the forgotten memory.

I told Philip, of course, and he patiently listened to the strange recollection; unable, I feel, to remember it himself. He was, after all, wrestling with his own demons - having witnessed far more than I would care to imagine as far as UFO's were concerned - and I was frustrated at the lack of detail following the encounter with the whitish-beige entity.

Why had it come all those years ago? What did it want of me? And why didn't it speak?

There was no telepathy on its part either, which is so commonly reported by abductees, and I did not even see a spaceship. Nevertheless, I could not recall the missing time which invariable took place.

If the encounter, and just the encounter, was triggered by a freak accident - and which transpired after a good twenty years - then how on earth can the missing time ever be accounted for?

I refuse to consider hypnosis, in the likelihood that I should unwittingly elaborate the incident. If it has taken twenty years for me to recall this much, then perhaps another twenty - and following an additional freak mishap - might just jog the little grey-cells enough to furnish me with the rest.

Would I really like to know? "Curiosity," so the old saying goes, "killed the cat!"

Whatever this creature was, it had evidently managed - with expert precision - to mask all traces of its interaction with me at the time. The brain is, after all, a complex biological computer, though it would seem that the alien was masterful enough in controlling certain aspects of my very own.

Wouldn't that suggest to you that this so-commonly-reported-species has a supreme understanding of us? This raises a very interesting conclusion.

They have been here for a very long time; enough, at the very least, to warrant manipulating aspects of our consciousness on a cunning level.

Chapter Three

The Grinning Dog & the Cheshire Cat

Since recalling this incident, along with witnessing incredible sightings much later in life, I slowly began to wonder why it was that both Philip and I - more than not - had diverse encounters. Philip, by the way, has documented his own in his book 'BELIEVE' and which is published by Capall Bann.

This intriguing question left me wondering as to why, until I finally hit on a possible theory. I will share this with you in a moment.

Returning to the Bignell estate, another oddity plagued Mum to the point of actually taking action, and she has relayed this event to me on more than one occasion. As a matter of fact, the phenomenon has reoccurred throughout our numerous moves and which is still happening to this very day. Philip and I shared a room upstairs in the cottage, and it was - like the others - extensive. During winter or when it was cold, Mum would light the fire before putting us to bed, tucking us in and returning downstairs for the night.

But, she would become annoyed to hear us running about and causing a ruckus. The cottage, as I said, was detached and a modest distance away from the mansion itself, and so noise pollution was virtually absent. She would race upstairs to give us a good telling off - as you would expect - only to find us still tucked up in our beds, fast asleep. This was a usual occurrence and one which baffled Mum.

It would appear that we had visitors upstairs; either crafty ones who disappeared at the first hint of detection ... or invisible ones! I often wonder, at this point, whether the creature I saw in the garden had returned, along with friends; intent on doing whatever it was it did.

We left the Bignell property a few years later, having to give Prince to a local farm, before moving to South Africa in 1976. Eighteen months later, we returned to England; living in Tatchbrook Road, Middlesex , with our Grandparents for a while, before moving to Luton.

* * *

I think that High School was the worst experience of our lives; being twins, for the simple fact that children and teenagers can be cruel. Anything odd or out of the ordinary represents a threat to them and so they retaliate by abusive name-lobbing.

The years following 1980 were, for us, as daunting as they were to become a virtual prison sentence, along with the next four years of our arduous trials at the High School in which we attended and of which I shall not name. It resided in Luton, quite a distance away from our house in Hazlebury Crescent; being a modest, detached Victorian dwelling situated on a road that wound up to the Luton Town Football Club.

Don't get me wrong, we shared happy times there too - away from school, that is - though the misery we endured from the callous pupils, who banded together to alienate us, was rather profound.

Upon enrolling at the dreaded High School the teachers decided that it would be in our best interests if we were separated; each attending different Form groups. Because we have always been so close, I was mortified at being thrust into classes without my better half to support me and this only added to the cruel jibes which the pupils, having already defined us as oddities, threw at me.

Philip also found himself under attack and this insufferable torment lasted four years, the final one thankfully being somewhat tranquil and more civil, with most of the tormentors having left.

It was this separation that recently gave me an insight into our diverse UFO encounters. The teacher's decision was based solely, I feel, on thwarting us from sharing knowledge and fearing repercussions when the exams finally raised their ugly heads. In a way, perhaps the aliens - or whatever they are - wished to prevent clarification on a similar scale and so, like the teachers, had us separated. It certainly seems to make sense, if my assumption is to be believed.

Those harrowing times, I am sure, prompted Spirit to give us a message of hope when we were just 12 years old, and it came through Philip one day while out playing near the old railway line, just across the road from our house. And Philip, I add with pride, is now an award-winning medium.

At the time, I did not wholly believe in an afterlife, let alone spiritual entities who occupied it. And, as for aliens ... well, you could have kissed them goodbye!

"We are going to write books," he told me, sitting on an old wooden gate adjacent to the line. "Also, we will see the Queen and appear on TV."

Those were his exact words and I did recall feeling somewhat star struck by them, because it was so out of character for him to pronounce such things. Needless to say, and on reflection, I now understand that Spirit - those wonderful souls residing in Heaven - were broadcasting a message of hope and which did, as a matter of fact, eventually all come true. They must have been aware of our young trepidations regarding life in general, and set about offering a small glimpse of the future.

This was shortly before I had two more bizarre encounters with extra-terrestrials that were, I am quite certain, masking their tracks by initiating terrifying visions to cloud the events; ensuring that I did not recognise their hand in the matter.

Nonetheless, their smart tactics failed during the latter, because I remembered seeing their faces. Unfortunately, they had wittingly masked themselves and, if any form of amnesia had been initiated after the encounter, I must have consciously fought it; shattering the illusion. The year was 1982.

With the first encounter, I was sound asleep in my bed when, quite by chance, I awoke; feeling rather unsettled for some peculiar reason. As I sat up, I had no idea what time it was, other than it being dark outside. I don't recall either Philip or I possessing a clock until the following year, and my watch was on my desk, next to my home computer - a Sinclair ZX81 - which I was learning to programme and which I was excelling in rather swiftly.

There was something sitting in the corner of the room and, as I strained to look, I was horrified to notice that it was a dog. This dog was not real - I knew that instantly - because it was actually grinning back at me. Its eyes were red, along with the unscrupulous smirk it so unkindly wore. I could see the neatly brushed fur on its head and neck being blackish-brown, though was baffled at how I could distinguish such things in the dark!

I was terrified and could not even scream; my eyes instinctively locked on it to ensure that it did not budge a centimetre. All that was going through my head, at that precise moment, was where the hell the light switch was, in case I should have to sprint for it. It was this harrowing thought that led to another startling realisation.

In some strange way, the room was distorted and I could not, for the life of me, gauge my bearings. I merely stared back at this demonic thing - this intruder that had nestled itself quite assuredly in my room - and wondered who was going to make the first move.

Now, I must stress to you at this point that it was not a dream or nightmare; although the rational-minded scientist, psychologist or UFO debunker would happily pass it off as either one or the other. Just how this dreadful scenario ended, I have no idea, because I awoke in my bed in the morning, feeling somewhat anxious and strangely vulnerable.

It was the calm before the storm!

A few nights later, I had an even more petrifying experience, and one which led me to understand just what I was up against. To put it bluntly; when you have no control over a power that is beyond your wildest dreams, you are at its mercy.

Again, I was in bed, sound asleep. I awoke in the dead of night, due to the darkness to abruptly find myself descending from the sky. It was the most harrowing experience to date and, as I dropped, I could see the star spangled heavens. I remembered having the distinct impression of being over our house, and my intuition was aptly justified as I effortlessly drifted through the loft towards by bedroom.

I was staring up all the time, the disconcerting sensation of rapidly falling reminding me of a rollercoaster ride when the car makes a dive, and I recalled every hair on my body standing on end. In a sense, it was as though an electrical charge was surging through me.

It was then when I saw something staring back down at me from above!

The head of a grinning Cheshire cat, similar to the character that featured in the Lewis Carole book 'Alice in Wonderland,' was beaming at me; its smirk never faltering. The fur on its head was grey, with intermittent black streaks running through it and, as I examined it in depth, there followed a slight bump. I had arrived back in my bed. After that, the cat disappeared.

I recalled shaking with fear, pulling the covers up over me and trying to work out what exactly had transpired. I was absolutely terrified and remembered feeling cold - strangely exposed - and these feelings did not dissolve until I finally fell asleep.

A few days later, it all came back to me. I am certain that I was not meant to recall the incident but, by a fluke - and while I was eating my sandwiches at school during the lunch hour - it simply popped into my head without any conscious effort on my part. It was as casual as a thought.

Although the grinning dog episode has never, to this day, been uncovered, the latter event was quite revealing!

I was in a hospital, but knew instinctively that it was not a real hospital, and this infirmary - I was absolutely certain - was in the sky. There were no windows present, and no doors from what I could discern, though a sterile atmosphere engulfed the area. I could see a bed in the centre of the room, along with a multitude of daunting-looking tools lying on a movable workbench nestled beside it.

I was in a wheelchair.

"Hello, Ronald," a male voice called. I immediately turned to my right and saw a tall man standing over me. He was dressed in bluish overalls, complete with a white mask concealing his mouth, together with a sanitary hairnet. I knew at that very moment - upon viewing him - that he was not a real man at all, but an impostor. There was something false about him - something amiss - though his soothing words and composed nature eased me a little; if only a little, due to him possessing a degree of confidence. "We are going to perform some tests on you."

Any reassurance I might have felt briskly evaporated and I began to sob as he wheeled my chair towards the formidable-looking bed I had come to understand as being an operating table.

"Please, I don't want an operation."

I remembered saying these exact words and, as we approached the table, three heavily-clad nurses - their faces concealed by hygiene masks - briskly came into view. They merely nodded to me and I remembered thinking how odd it was that I had not seen them before. I merely put it down to the shock of having been thrust so unmercifully into a medical situation I knew nothing about. I was certain that there was nothing wrong with me to warrant executing these so-called 'tests.'

We stopped just short of the table and, very gently, the doctor leaned over me.

"You will not be harmed in any way," he promised, resuming his posture before approaching the formidable-looking workbench. He selected one of the tools. "These tests are for your own good. As I said, you will not be harmed."

His tone held such conviction that I recalled having no choice but to cooperate. The tool he held was not like a syringe, but a peculiar looking oblong thing that had a large nodule poking out at one end. He brought it down to my right hand and then gently pressed it onto my skin.

I must have blanked out because, after that, I remembered plummeting, with the star-spangled heavens besieging me, only to view the uncanny Cheshire cat who graced me with his accursed grin; a mocking testament, perhaps, to my vulnerability and powerless demeanour with these people who, I suspected, were not people at all; but medical practitioners from another world.

Chapter Four

Delusions of Grandeur

It is startling for me to realise that, back then, and following the harrowing recollections of the grinning dog, the Cheshire cat and the strange doctor, I was in denial. Whether it was based on fear, or my own personal ignorance, I am not sure, though I am certain of one thing; this topic was highly controversial. At the time, many magazines were published, exploring the validity of people's alleged experiences with UFOs and apparent extra-terrestrial contact.

Philip was heavily into the subject and, upon borrowing dozens of UFO magazines from a kind teacher who lectured at the High School we attended, he digested many of the accounts out of curiosity. I couldn't help but express a mild interest in the subject myself and so, during the course of a summer holiday, spent a good deal of time reading through them.

I did try to maintain an open mind, but there again; had to weigh up the odds upon reading some of the stories that were printed in them ... one of which had me literally screaming with laughter.

I read an account whereby a man was purported to have been given pancakes made for him by a visiting alien. The tears were streaming down my face as I wondered where it was this friendly creature had acquired the recipe and if he was a master chef back home on his planet; having developed the art of concocting desserts to give as peace-offerings to his fellow human buddies.

Of course, there are ludicrous notions which people believe to the point of astonishment and, having pored through many books regarding the subject, I have made a personal assessment of the good, the bad and the ugly. It is strange, but I seem to have developed a modest record of judging fact from fiction; wholeheartedly trusting my instincts because, for me, many of the accounts did not ring true. As a matter of fact, a few of them were downright preposterous and insulting.

Pancakes!

I'm sorry if I sound rather harsh, but I can safely say that I am not without regret with what I have surmised regarding this particular incident, and it is not a heartless backlash either. Let's face it; you do get sensationalists out there, along with your fair share of cuckoos.

Nowadays, photographic evidence is far more complex and convincing, with the use of computer generated images - both static and motion - flooding the likes of the media world. Unfortunately, this has muddied the pool for truthful researchers who are now besieged by state-of-the-art, Hollywood-style effects and which leave them virtually scratching their heads.

One thing I have discovered about this topic; when you take one step forward, you invariably take two steps back!

I was, however, certain about one alleged and famous UFO contactee being a hoaxer regarding his alleged encounters in the past. I had read one of his books out of inquisitiveness and knew, after evaluating it, that he was an out-and-out sham; and this travesty only incensed me to the point of infuriation. I was not laughing then, but downright livid at the twaddle he so convincingly and expertly spun. As it happened, Philip also agreed with my views. We were beginning to find that this topic was swamped with a good dose of embellishment, and that's putting it mildly.

As a matter of fact, I was staggered at how, after examining the photographic evidence he supplied, people actually fell for it when his books reached the shelves. One of the static shots depicts him unconvincingly sitting within a cigar-shaped vehicle while in flight, happily peering out of a dodgy window. Firstly, he cannot be sitting because, judging from the angle, the base of the ship is too short to accommodate a chair; he would have to be kneeling, or lying flat. Also, the aliens must have been experts with his camera to afford such a snap, having followed his ship; thus angling it to catch him through their very own porthole.

It also angers me when fans report - knowing that the photographs were faked - that he had fixed them merely to add emphasis to his assertions. One woman was utterly obsessed with the man - to the point of painting portraits of him, along with his Ufonaughts - and would not tolerate any negative views concerning his testimony. We had to endure listening to audio tapes made by him while attending her UFO club, whereby he explained how he patiently waited the arrival of his alien friend's spaceship, to the refreshing taste of Coca Cola! I most certainly would not be enjoying any kind of beverage in the presence of an otherworldly craft upon arrival, let alone casually swigging it back before creatures from another planet disembarked.

Another incident left me virtually speechless!

One American woman - we recall seeing on TV while pursuing this phenomenon - was purported to have been taken to the moon by bald headed men; whereupon she, along with her merry band, broke out into a dance; with her kicking up the lunar dust in jovial excitement beside the parked flying saucer, while observing the Earth gracefully turning on its axis.

It beggars belief!

And, before you consider me to be a hypocrite - which I am not - let me shortly explain to you what happened following this assessment. I think you will agree, by then, that I was mentally challenged to record my very own events; along with Philip, as well as having to separate the good apples from the bad ones.

*   *   *

Philip and I are truthful. We are also highly imaginative, like many others. Now, considering both these facets, you may start to wonder how it is that one can be truthful regarding a topic such as this, as well as being highly imaginative. Some people would argue that it is a contradiction in itself because imagination, for all its wonderment, could very well play a major part with the likes of us concocting realistic visions of otherworldly contact.

Well, let me start by saying that, with psychologically sound people, imagination cannot derive and project unearthly creatures, or scenarios, to the point of audibly and visually receiving them in the physical sense. This would be an insulting conjecture to a great many millions for the simple fact that it implies that their minds must surely be unstable; somehow casting realistic events out into the open. And, even if this were the case, it cannot scientifically be done.

This also covers daydreaming.

If you try and mentally conceive a car right now in your mind, you may very well see an aspect of it; or a hazy interpretation at the very least. And, if you try harder, it does not come as a picture in a sense; but as a vague construal.

Now, can you imagine your car being projected out before your very eyes, by the will of your imagination, to the point of seeing it as a fully-fledged, three dimensional object with the clarity you would expect of the real thing? The result, I am sure you will agree, is a testament to your kind experiment and one which I am sure illustrates my argument quite aptly.

But what about dreams during sleep - when the brain activity is tranquil - and your subconscious mind is free to grapple with irrepressible visions, episodes and a million other extraordinary things that perhaps interest, trouble or taunt you on a daily basis?

Dreams, though fantastically real - and which certainly do have an extraordinary clarity beyond any conscious method of visualisation we know - cannot be initiated unless one is asleep. And this, in itself, can be another insulting assumption made by family, friends and so-called experts, who insist that, if you happen to see something supernatural, then you were probably just dreaming. And, as I have already mentioned, children cannot imagine in the sense that we do; not from an early age.

This result is conclusive and warranted me to pursue both the psychic and UFO enigma with the clarity and respect that it deserved; when, of course, I had received enough signs to initiate such research.

*   *   *

In my mid-twenties, I had seen enough strange objects in the sky, that could not be explained, to openly embrace the topic, albeit cautiously. Having read a ground-breaking book by an American author, based on his personal trials with an extra-terrestrial intelligence (the name of which I cannot mention due to the proceeding events) we discovered that he - or rather his colleagues - ran a mailing service, which was designed for the likes of us, and many others, to share our own experiences - once put on a list - that was distributed to the UFO disciples in America.

Before I proceed with this, I must categorically state that the author in question had no control over the letters sent and received on behalf of the interested parties. His book, by the way, was extraordinary and, on a personal note, I believed him.

Philip and I began to receive letters from a good deal of Americans, which was charming; all eager to share their own experiences with us regarding their alien encounters. Some were genuine while others dubious. As the years passed, we found the communications to become somewhat fanciful; blatantly revealing cracks as to the validity of otherworldly contact. As a result of this, the-said testimonies were put into question.

Here is an example of one of the UFO disciple's letters. I have only slightly distorted it to protect us from repercussions, though I grant you that the material is relevant to what was actually written.

Hi Phil and Ronnie,

I dream of having alien babies every day. I want one of these bald-headed creatures to fall in love with me, for us to marry, and to have many alien kids. I can't stop thinking about this and the days that pass get harder and harder because I am waiting for my space lover to arrive and to take me in his arms.

And this was just one of many! Privately, the whole letter-thing was becoming an absolute charade and so, regrettably, Philip and I decided to have our names removed from the list and to terminate all links with these troubled souls. I have to say that I did not laugh at the contents of these letters, but adopted a more civil approach; though I was livid at having to swallow such trivia and swearing to myself that a more careful approach to the subject was required.

How on Earth could I study and record my own peculiar events with the likes of such distractions? If these people were relaying their letters to so many others - with some of them having been photocopied for just such a purpose - it implied to me that the subject was not being approached in a judicious manner.

Could people really take these accounts seriously? Certainly, and apart from the latter, there were enough accounts published in books and magazines to warrant genuine attention, though I remembered thinking to myself, at the time, that the entire issue regarding UFO's was not only being elaborated upon, mocked and damaged by such ludicrous notions, but that it was also adding fuel to the fire as far as debunkers were concerned.

This journey, I discovered, was like walking through a minefield!

*   *   *

Going back in time a little, I would like to tell you about Grandma King, her psychic gift and of the peculiar UFO we saw in her garden. Because UFO's and Spirituality are pigeonholed into separate boxes, I now understand that they may share a common denominator, as I take a trip down memory lane which eventually unfolded into a remarkable turn of events; finally opening my eyes to the larger picture of our world and, indeed, our place in the universe.

Chapter Five

"Your Grandma knows all...!"

The long summer holidays for us, back in the 1980's, were heavenly. At the Hazlebury Crescent house in Luton, Philip and I would excitedly pack all our toys and things into black plastic sacks, eager to leave for Feltham, Middlesex, whereupon our Mother would take us to stay with Grandma and Granddad King for a full six weeks. We both loved it in Feltham, because Grandma and Granddad spoilt us rotten.

Of course, we were never denied anything from Mum, and she always made sure - along with our beloved Granddad Kinsella - that we, and our sister Chris, had the latest innovations of the time. But, Grandma King made an extra-special point of selflessly bestowing the very best on us.

Upon arrival, Grandma would appear in the doorway of their moderately sized three-story house. Her immaculate grey hair, brushed back to form orderly waves, together with a sensible blouse and skirt, greeted us in the fashion of a Queen. There was always the smell of pastries wafting down the hallway from the kitchen as Grandma was an avid cook; having prepared apple pie, rock cakes, bread pudding to name but a few. Upon giving her a hug, the aroma of these exotic desserts were overpowered by her adored and favourite perfume Youth Dew.

Even at thirteen, we towered over her, because she was petite. Granddad would welcome us with a more unpreten-tious

41

GRANDMA KING

PAINTED BY THE ARTIST SUSAN D. O'CONNOR (WITH KIND PERMISSION)

handshake - because he was respectfully of the old school. He'd laugh at us as we hastily showed them both our latest toys before getting as far as the sitting-room; not waiting to settle. Being a tall man, he normally peered at us both through his reading glasses, as he more-often-than-not had his head in a book.

Tatchbrook Road, where their house resided, was - from what I can remember - a long and tidy one, with theirs being at the very end and next to a stream. On Saturday mornings, and during our stay with them, they'd stuff £5.00 notes into our pockets, knowing that Philip and I enjoyed visiting the bargain bookshop in Hounslow. We'd leave the house, with Grandma continually reminding us, "Don't talk to strangers," and, "Use the Green Cross Code." This was at a time when mobile phones were nonexistent.

She'd keep a vigilant eye on us both as we walked up the long road until we were out of eyeshot, before re-entering the house where, we're sure, she'd fret until we returned.

Those summer holidays were the best that time could supply. We'd sit for hours with Grandma in the spacious sitting-room, with Granddad having been packed off to work at Heathrow Airport, talking about life, the future and our dreams at becoming writers. Having seen a science fiction feature film called '*The Black Hole*' in 1979 at the Odeon Cinema in Luton, a friend of ours had bought us the soundtrack on LP by Disneyland Records and which was composed by the brilliant, John Barry. During the 80's, we'd bring this record along with us to play on Granddad's expensive record deck; fascinated by the sinister themes which Grandma quite humourously quoted as being, 'The Death March.' No matter what we liked, she'd allow us to pursue it while at the Tatchbrook residence, and we'd dust her house and vacuum the carpets with '*The Black Hole*' playing out at full blast, inspiring us with futuristic visions of space travel and impressive robots.

Grandma would often kick her legs up into the air during the chores, singing to herself and being quite theatrical. After that, it was tea and cakes, quite literally!

Now, there was something that Philip and I didn't quite know about Grandma at the time, though she gave subtle hints as to the gift she possessed. And, I have to say, even then, it didn't quite twig.

Grandma was psychic!

One summer, I had bruises on my left leg which were concealed by my slacks and, upon entering the house for the long stay; she took me into the kitchen and told me to roll up my left trouser leg.

"I thought as much," she said, examining the bruises. I stared at her incredulously. "Grandma, how did you know that?" She gave me a wise look, tapping her nose with a meaningful finger and replying: "Ah, but your Grandma knows all!"

I was thunderstruck and recalled shaking my head, though that admission was the first of many. Because the family never spoke about Grandma being psychic - with both Philip and I completely ignorant of the subject at the time - we did not understand exactly what being 'psychic' meant. We badgered her for answers as she revealed more evidence in the form of past events concerning us and which she was not privy to.

"The fairies down the bottom of the garden whisper things to me," she said. "They tell your Grandma everything."

At dusk, when our Grandparents were watching television in the sitting room, we'd go out into the garden and search for these alleged fairies of Grandma's that told her everything; never once capturing one of these diminutive-winged-beauties. Our hopes of gaining secrets from them dwindled as we called out to them each night; sneaking over the rockery and hunting in every nook and cranny, to no avail.

* * *

My first recollection of what a medium was happened at Grandma's house and on TV. As I said, Philip and I were not educated on this phenomenon and so we sniggered behind Grandma's back as she watched the programme with avid interest; with the medium giving a live demonstration of clairvoyance to an audience.

This distinguished woman was also a notable author who had written work based on her experiences, though we did not appreciate her gift at the time, and so whispered nasty little things about her to ourselves as she set about proving to her enthralled viewers that the spirit world was real and that their loved-ones were waiting to communicate.

"Load of old trash!" I said. "She's a fake."

Because the Medium was world-renowned, Grandma gave me a book written by her - just one - and, being the courteous young man that I was, I accepted it graciously; promising to read it when I got home. Nonetheless, I stuffed it on my bookshelf where it collected dust; never once turning a solitary page.

I did not know at the time that the book was to return to haunt me, and that the wake-up call I got from spirit was to show me, unwaveringly, that the Medium was indeed genuine. My personal ignorance would be swayed by a tragedy; a tragedy that involved Grandma and, ironically, it was her who kindly, but curtly, put me in my place by a brilliant Medium of whom I had a sitting with, when she finally departed this world.

* * *

In Grandma's garden a year or so later, some members of the family had gathered for dinner. The men had gone out - whether down to the pub or play golf, I can't remember - though I do recall us in the back garden at around midday, or thereafter ... the women talking as usual amongst themselves and preparing dinner; our beloved Mother assisting with the chores. The weather was beautiful with not a cloud in the sky.

Philip and I were playing in the back garden when, quite suddenly, something casually descended towards us. It was a small silver ball - a perfect sphere with no distinguishable seams on it at all - and it dropped so low, it must have halted around 25-30 feet in the air. At first, we thought it was a balloon but, from what I can remember, it was much smaller and did not flail about which is so characteristic of balloons.

In any case, balloons don't drop, unless they lose helium or are temporarily forced down by a gust.

It simply hung suspended over us for a considerable amount of time - not moving an inch - and this caused me to become extremely unnerved. Upon greater inspection, I could not see a knot beneath it to suggest it had a tie to contain the gas, nor a dangling cord, either - absolutely nothing! In fact, it appeared completely solid.

"Grandma, what is it?" Philip asked. The reply from her was even more bizarre. "It's the fairies," she said. "They've come to take a closer look at us."

For her to come out with a statement like that only validated the strangeness of the thing and, as I fixed it within my sights - never once taking my eyes off it - the women tried to hit it with a lengthy wooden washing pole. But, it could not be reached.

After a while, it began to move again, heading towards the house and then climbing adjacent with it; reaching the roof. The way it flew was uncanny and we agreed that it seemed to be controlled; skimming the top with perfect precision (neither wavering nor bouncing) as it disappeared to the other side.

I recalled us diving inside the house and scrambling up the open-spiral staircase in the hallway, only to burst into Grandma's bedroom on the first floor to observe it through the windows overlooking the street. We watched as it steadily flew over the road before disappearing into the distance.

Personally, I doubted 'the fairy' explanation because, even at that age, I reasoned that these small, magical beings did not fly about in such fanciful vehicles as silver balls. However, I suspected that it was probably some type of probe, or electronic camera, and that it was to do with extra-terrestrials. Don't ask me why, but that was the first impression I got and this thought surprised me as much as Grandma's own statement.

*　　*　　*

If Grandma's declaration at being psychic - though subtly put - was bewildering enough, then Granddad's confessional remark on the supernatural was even more bizarre!

Philip and I had visited our beloved bargain-bookshop in Hounslow again, where we purchased a hardback about poltergeists for around £3.00. You may wonder why it was that we scoffed at Mediums, though expressed interest in more demonic affairs. I can't answer that wholly, though I think it may have had something to do with our own curiosity and Hollywood, who were releasing films based on Poltergeists and other dark entities at the time. Besides, there were plenty of movies back then concerning the forces of evil, and so we wanted to explore stories that might relate to them in a fanciful way. Upon returning home to Tatchbrook, with the prized purchase in Philip's hand, Granddad was none too happy upon us showing him the sleeve.

"Get rid of it!" he demanded, staring through his reading glasses perched on the end of his nose. "Burn it, if you have to."

"But why, Granddad?"

"You don't bloody well mess with the likes of them, that's why!" he retorted. "Just get rid of it!"

We were both shocked by his outburst and quickly replaced the book in the supplied brown paper bag, taking it upstairs and putting it to one side. We rarely saw Granddad get angry - and Grandma never - and his words sent chills up our spines. Later on, and having simmered, he actually admitted to us that he believed in the supernatural; though specifically made a harsh point for us never to tamper with it - ever!

"Don't meddle with things you don't understand, sons," he warned over the dinner table, wagging his fork at us. "You'll regret it if you do."

Was he aware that the fairies down the bottom of the garden actually talked with Grandma? Wasn't that, in itself, supernatural? We daren't challenge him over it just in case Grandma kept her meetings with them secret. We didn't want him taking a tin of paraffin, along with a match, to set fire to them upon discovering their hideout!

Being that we respected Granddad, we decided to do as he jolly well asked. As soon as we returned to Hazlebury Crescent, we set light to the book outside and in Dad's old wheelbarrow, burying the ashes in the garden. We then wrote and told Grandma, informing Granddad, that we had got rid of the book as instructed.

For a man who never openly expressed his views on the topic, Granddad did confess to us that he also believed that the great pyramids in Egypt were not built by men, but by Alien Gods, who arrived thousands of years ago to lend a hand in teaching humans about architecture, agriculture and science; whereby they were consecrated and incidentally worshipped.

It would seem that our extra-terrestrial friends, or foes, have been around for a very long time, if Granddad's assumptions are to be believed, and as I delved further into the subject, I found remarkable evidence - by leading researchers - that lends credence to this very notion.

I was also to discover, in my early thirties, that I myself, along with Philip, interacted with these space creatures' centuries ago and that this confession - as fantastic as it sounds - may very well symbolise a harmony between both the alien and spiritual phenomena. Indeed, Philip has made his own conclusions regarding 'The Grey's' in his book 'BELIEVE,' though the extra-terrestrials of the past are not, I suspect, 'Grays.'

These creatures I mention are, I believe, even more ancient; being, I suspect, masterful overlords that governed 'The Grays' for a reason I shall disclose towards the end of the book, whereby I have made a few conclusions of my own.

And this hypothesis of mine might very well explain the very genesis of mankind, because the ancient ones I mention were - and still are - masters of genetic engineering, along with being pioneers of international manipulation.

LORD 'PROFESSOR' HAROLD

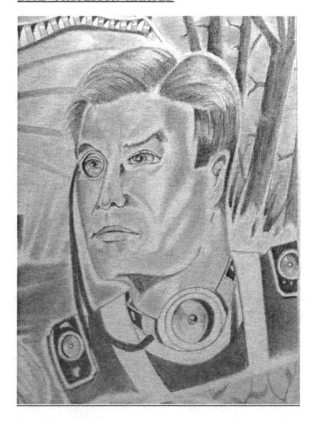

Chapter Six

The Third Wish

During the 80's and 90's, Philip and I were concentrating on writing, to try and break into the literary market. Because we always had a natural flair for drawing, we decided to fuse the two together by developing humourous children's books; working on detailed illustrations to accompany them. This ambition was not based on us merely trying to get published. Philip and I were always imaginative and had, through the years, developed characters which we thought would hopefully appeal to children; though they were not children themselves.

Two such characters, whom still remain very dear to us, are Lord 'Professor' Harold and Lady Alexandra. Philip and I created these in the mid 80's and during happier times in our lives, which encompassed freedom and creativity. Embracing this welcomed independence, we developed an alternative world within the pages of lined exercise books. As a result, two rivals both being wealthy beyond measure and living in Grand and stately homes, were born; clashing in adventures that were, I feel, the origins of our literary exploits.

Lord 'Professor' Harold was a dashing young man (being astute though pompous) who created state-of-the-art robots and machinery. His character reflected a sense of elegant pride, along with a damaging arrogance, and he'd flaunt his ingenious know-how before the people of this world - including the lovely Lady Alexandra - with aristocratic aplomb. Lady Alexandra, we felt, secretly admired the nobleman, though

LADY ALEXANDRA

she would stand up to him when the occasion arose. Being a somewhat gentle and understanding soul, she collided with the Professor on many occasions; one such escapade illustrating the fact that she wished to compete in 'The Grand National horse race' in an effort to achieve something worthy in her life. However, the crafty old peer could not be seen to lose his high-status and unchallenged superiority and so decides to compete along with her; building a tireless and super-fast mechanical horse, disguised as a genuine stallion. Water, of all things, ends up being his downfall in this particular story; with the horse ultimately malfunctioning and exploding prior to a water jump.

The Professor, so it turned out, fled with his tail between his legs, to the rapturous applause of Lady Alexandra's family. She, on the other hand, pitied him; her undying love never wavering and her heart fluttering in the secret hope that they would meet again; albeit on another adventure and during, no doubt, another clash!

I wonder, as I write this based on these particular characters, whether Philip and I were wishing to actually live these alternative worlds; with aristocratic people possessing wealth and status and high-intelligence? Certainly, they seemed to ooze from our imaginations with ease, with us frantically scribbling down such yarns and illustrating them; if only to read to one another and to see who could make the other one laugh the most.

We didn't know it at the time, but this was the first stage of a serious commitment. Our ambitious drive was being nurtured by such fanciful and inventive dreams. I am now convinced that it was Spirit's gift to us, combined with the unqualified progress of drawing and painting, and that, even back then, we were instinctively sowing the seeds for future interest.

As it happens, we met a kindly woman by the name of Eileen M. Pickering who was an established author herself (having written many western books under the name of Mark Falcon and which were published by Black Horse Western - Robert Hale Ltd) and she took an immediate interest in Professor Harold and Lady Alexandra. Running a quarterly publication entitled 'Writers Own Magazine,' she set about printing some of our short stories and encouraging us with our work, before deciding to publish a chronicle based on the Professor in 'Professor Harold & Co' in 1988. This was followed two years later by 'Lady Alexandra & Co,' both being fully illustrated. It was our first initial break and, though they came under a cottage-industry-imprint, this dear and loving woman inspired us with everything we did.

On a note of interest, I have recently modernised both Lord 'Professor' Harold and Lady Alexandra; my illustrations of them based on a keenness to bring them back one day and when time permits. It is interesting to note (as you kindly observe the pictures within the covers of this book) that they somehow - even now - denote a sense of antiquated style mixed with a contemporary edge; a fashion which I have tried to avoid but cannot seem to break away from. In some way, it is as though I have embraced past and present and I wonder if this is a reflection of my inner self; my soul? It is a fascinating conjecture.

Eileen eventually advised us to try the bigger publishing houses in London and so, accepting her guidance, we set about doing just that.

It was, to say the least, an arduous task, and we were never disillusioned at how cutthroat the market actually was, even back then. We sent our work out in countless brown envelopes, always remembering to enclose return postage; submitting sample illustrations along with a few chapters to both literary agents and publishers in England and America.

The editor of one major publishing company in the UK (Transworld) kindly sent Philip and I two free copies of a type of 'Dungeons and Dragons' book, which they had just released, along with a letter thanking us for our submission; though they were unable to pursue it at the time. I had sent them an illustration, and the editor told me that her art department had pinned it up on their notice board. It was an incredible honour and we were immensely grateful to the publishing company for their extremely kind encouragement and generosity.

Nonetheless, the rejection slips began to mount, though we were stubborn and would not give up. Little did we realise that it would take us until 2006 to jointly discover publishers for our work. We received moderate success eight years prior to this with an e-book published by the then, Puff-Adder Books. It was run by two women who expressed immediate interest in our coloured paintings, along with a story that centred around the antics of a super-hero dog, 'Magnus the Micro-Mutt' which we had copyrighted back in 1993. I had to reluctantly terminate the contract with them, having discovered a professional local agent (or so I thought) it was heart rending for me to do so, the agent was adamant and pulled all my strings, so-to-speak; wanting total control over the dog. Total! That was an under-statement. She ended up ripping us off, though we settled the score - if only to secure the rights to Magnus - and had to borrow, what was for me, a substantial sum of money from the bank to pay her off due to being threatened with legal action.

I remembered thinking that Philip and I were hard-up struggling to maintain a dream, and it didn't help matters when the so-called professional agent wrote us one last damaging letter to revel in her justification in wishing to exclusively own the copyright prior to obtaining the payoff; clearly expressing the fact that, because she could not hold the rights to Magnus, we would invariably suffer if we did not

MAGNUS THE MICRO-MUTT

The mechanical dog created by both Philip and myself in 1993 to offer a new vision for children.

CAPTAIN BAILEY, MAGNUS & THE PRINCESS

These were gifts from Spirit and which inspired us to
develop alternative worlds.

bow to a greater power. The only power we'd bow to is that of the Queen, God bless her, and I had no choice but to swallow my pride and settle the dispute. As it happened, she had done this before to other clients ... the poor souls! You live and you learn, so they say.

However, all was not as negative as it seemed at the time. Dame Barbara Cartland, the international best-selling romantic novelist , accepted our gifts of the-then self-published *'Magnus the Micro-Mutt'* books, encouraging us both (throughout the numerous years of communication) to carry on and promising to read the stories which she said 'were cleverly done!' She even tried to help us into the commercial world by suggesting we try her own literary agents. They declined, on the basis that they rightly did not handle children's fiction, though the enormous support this sweet, kind-hearted lady gave us was, without doubt, a huge boost during the harrowing times of finding one's feet and improving one's skills. She was an angel.

It was during this mammoth battle to find commercial interest that we had a bitter pill to swallow. Grandma was dying of cancer! I shall never forget the telephone call she made to us shortly before she passed and, upon speaking to her myself, she made me promise three things. The year was 1997 and it was approaching August.

"Ronnie, I'm dying," she simply told me on the phone. I was brave, nonetheless, and told her that I knew. "I want you to promise me three things, Loves."

"I'll try, Grandma," I replied.

"Firstly, concentrate on your writing. Never give up. Secondly, look after your Mother."

I promised these two things immediately, vowing to keep my word and assuring Grandma that she would have nothing to fear as far as they were concerned.

"My third wish is also important, Loves."

"What is it, Grandma?"

"Don't cry at my funeral. I am simply going home."

I didn't quite know how to respond to this, though I did tell her that I could not guarantee the third wish. It was the last time I actually spoke to Grandma and, when we got a phone call in the early hours of the morning, some time later, we knew that she had given up her battle with cancer. I broke down and cried.

Nonetheless, an extraordinary event occurred and which categorically proved, beyond a shadow of a doubt, that Grandma - with all her love and wisdom - was to unwaveringly secure her third wish without question. It sounds rather pompous - doesn't it - to think that I should receive special treatment from a lady who was loved by all; though I gather that there must have been some kind of method to it and that, even now, it may have been implemented to help me open my eyes to the bigger picture; that Grandma was indeed returning home to a far Grander world.

* * *

Funerals are, as we all know, sombre affairs. The family had gathered in Street, Somerset, to pay homage to Grandma as her coffin was carried into the church. I remembered being aghast as to how small it actually was, as it was settled before the altar; being rather like that of a child's. Grandma was petite, I knew, but even so, it was tiny!

Everyone had assembled and, as the minister proceeded to celebrate Grandma's life, something unusual happened.

A thought entered by head. I saw, at that precise moment and with people conspicuously wiping tears from their eyes, a scene that caused me to laugh. I had to literally stuff my handkerchief over my mouth to pretend that I was in absolute grief; the tears of hilarity streaming down my face and, with the hankie masking my disgraceful conduct, it was enough - I felt sure - to fool the congregation that I was indeed mournful.

Recalling it now, the event was so bizarre; it could only have been implemented by Grandma. I would never dare laugh at a funeral because it is totally sacrilegious to do so and, besides, the scene was just so out of character for me to conjure; being that my beloved Grandmother was lying dead before us.

I saw, upon viewing the coffin, a vision of her pushing the lid up and back, before climbing out. She then turned to face Granddad.

"Sod this, Jim!" she said. "Pop the kettle on and let's have a cup of tea!"

My tears wouldn't stop rolling as I snorted into the handkerchief, trying with all my might to end this shameful behaviour. I clearly remembered feeling mortified and looking around to see if anyone had noticed, though they were respectfully concentrating on the service at hand, no doubt considering me to be inconsolable.

I was utterly powerless to stop it and knew enough to realise - at that point - what Grandma was actually doing. I even raised my head to observe the ceiling in confusion, unsuccessfully trying to gauge her spirit that was, I felt sure, watching the service.

After the ceremony, she was driven to the crematorium and I have to say, with hand on heart, that I did not shed one tear of grief.

She had secured her third wish with stunning perfection, forcing a smile on my face and reminding me that she had indeed gone home. This, in effect, opened my eyes to a larger picture; one which I had wrestled with and which had brought both bewilderment and a wretched sense of hope in my on-going battle with the supernatural.

* * *

If that sounds incredible, I was in for an absolute shock some years later and it was this, and ultimately this, that reduced my stagnant and dogmatic views to ashes and for me to embrace an understanding about us and our infinite universe.

I was also to discover that I had walked the Earth, along with Philip, thousands of years ago, and that the age-old empires of the past were very much factual. And, having covered this point, you will hear my testimony of interacting with extra-terrestrial beings referred to as 'The Gods' when they visited our world in a time, I believe, of prosperity and advancement, and who's dealings with us earned them the right of loyalty … and sacrifice.

Chapter Seven

The Reading

As it happened - and sometime after Grandma's funeral - Philip decided to see a Medium. I am so glad that he did because this, in turn, completely changed our lives. Of course, I jibed him over it, expecting him to be greeted by an old lady - perhaps of gipsy descendant - with a crystal ball on a table, in a shady little room that reeked 'false' in every sense. This sounds pessimistic on my part, I know, though truthfully I was developing a certain degree of respect towards the unknown; considering my personal experiences with UFOs which I expertly choose to forget at the time, along with the startling incident at the church.

However, the outcome of Philip's reading was nothing short of breathtaking.

The Medium's name was Penny, and Penny lived in Clapham at the time, though she conducted her readings in Bedford. She was not, as it turned out, an old lady of gipsy descent, but an attractive young woman who, we found out later, also worked her gift in the USA; especially for the police.

Upon returning that day from seeing the Medium, Philip appeared ashen but excited as he walked through the door. There was also something else which I immediately picked up … something so incredible it caused me to sit up and take note; I could smell Youth Dew all over him! In fact, it was so potent, it lingered in the air for hours and I knew, there and then, that Grandma had come to visit him. I was confused as to how a perfume could be replicated through 'ethereal contact' and asked him if Penny wore Youth Dew herself. He told me that she did not and that there was no perfume back at her place at all. I was flabbergasted.

When he relayed his reading to me, I was totally transported; shaking my head and wondering how on earth it was that the Medium could possibly know so much. On his journey to Penny's, Philip got lost and had to stop and ask two old ladies for directions; which they kindly supplied.

The first thing Penny said to him when he arrived, and upon opening the door, was:

"You had to stop and ask two old dears for directions, didn't you?"

He simply nodded in astonishment as she led him into the sitting room within the flat, and prepared him a drink before the reading. He settled himself down in a chair and was handed his drink, with Penny taking an opposite seat. She then turned to look slightly away from him as she acknowledged her Spirit Guide who, in turn, poured out his entire life to her; with Grandma arriving to be present with Philip during the session.

As it happened, she told him that he would become a working Medium himself, in the future, though Philip strongly challenged this, frankly admitting to her that he couldn't even raise the skin off a rice pudding. She was, nonetheless, adamant. She also knew that he was an identical twin, that we were writing books, that we lived together and-so-on; the reading having lasted two solid hours. On top of that, there was a man who came through from Spirit, and whom Philip did not know, and who was standing behind Grandma all along. Apparently, he had died drowning in the Navy at a very young age and was related to us, though Philip could not take the evidence; having no knowledge of him whatsoever.

Nonetheless, when this was relayed to the family, they informed him that it was Granddad's brother, Graham - Grandma having developed a friendship with him - who had indeed drowned at a young age while serving in the Navy.

Having digested everything he freshly relayed to me, I spent a few weeks mulling it over in my head before deciding to see Penny myself. Of course, I was extremely nervous. Philip said that she did not choose to see everyone; (having the spiritual knack of distinguishing people ready to pursue her gift just for material profit), but I was determined to have a reading.

I finally called Penny and she agreed to see me. I do recall, at the time, feeling comforted at having qualified over her 'material-profit-filter' she cleverly wielded and was excited, though cautious, all the same. For the first time in my life, I was to see a working medium, and in private.

* * *

The day arrived when I was to meet Penny at her home in Clapham. Because I could not drive, Philip insisted on taking me and I was grateful. He sat with me during the reading, because I was nervous. Before we left, I decided to wrap an illustration of mine up in a black plastic bag (I always paint on hard white card) depicting our robot dog character, 'Magnus the Micro-Mutt.' There was method to my madness, I assure you, and, with this tucked securely under my arm, we set off to see Penny.

On the way there, I made a mental note of blocking all thoughts and facial expressions while in the presence of the Medium, just to be absolutely certain that she could not read my mind, or gauge any reaction during the sitting. The 'mind reading bit,' I knew, could not have been possible, due to the simple fact of her having already brought through a relative of ours without Philip having any prior knowledge of him. I suppose you could say that I was trying to play safe.

When we arrived, I was greeted by an extremely distinct looking young woman and I couldn't get over how attractive she was - my big misconception of Mediums being either old or of Gipsy/Romany descendant - and she welcomed us into her sitting room. The first impression I got from her was that she was both honest and gentle; her warm smile and kind eyes settling any nerves I might have had. She made us both a drink before beginning the session. I placed my painting down beside my chair as she proceeded to take a seat before us, quietly summoning her Spirit Guide to the gathering.

"Please don't feel that I'm being rude if I look slightly away from you, Ronald," she reassured. "This is how I communicate with my Guide."

I was comfortable with that and told her so.

"You have two fathers, don't you," she casually informed, not making eye contact with me, but being intently focused on an invisible scene - or something like that - upon the wall behind me. "You also have a half sister."

I was impressed as she filled me in with their details, though I'm afraid to say that I cannot disclose certain aspects of the former due to sensitive issues and which would be unfair of me to do so. However, Penny saw the lot ... I was gob smacked!

"You are correct," I told her, impressed. "My goodness!"

"Someone's coming through, now," she informed. "It's your Grandma. Your Grandma died of cancer, though she's well and is now here and around you; stroking your hair. She has taken the cancer away from your family and, although you grieve for her, you must not. She tells me that you are the sensitive one of the two and that she has a special place in her heart for you, Ronald. She's standing before a man dressed in a Navy uniform, who tragically died by drowning at a young age. He has expressed interest in both you and your brother's work."

I said nothing, but knew the gentleman to be Granddad's brother, Graham. I could feel something around my head; as though hands were subtly brushing my hair. I wanted to run my fingers through it, to stop the disconcerting sensation I was receiving, but thought better of it in front of Penny.

"She gave you a book, didn't she, Ronald; one book by a renowned Medium," Penny continued. She then looked at me with a wry grin on her face. "Your Grandma's telling me that you haven't read it, you naughty boy. You must read it."

I was utterly stunned and I actually felt the blood drain from my face as she relayed this information to me. She was absolutely correct and I remembered feeling totally exposed to this incredible woman with her astonishing gift. My jaw must have been on the floor as she continued without distraction.

"You write children's and science fiction books, your Grandma's telling me," she said. "You are currently trying to find publishers for them. This will come in time. Also, a film deal will arrive and you must be prepared to swallow your pride, due to the fact that they will heavily alter the script. It will be, in any case, a stepping stone to greater things."

I turned to face Philip and he noticed my stunned expression as she carried on.

"You are a solitary soul, preferring your own company rather than others," she continued. "My Guide is showing me a scene of you working in your bedroom and is laughing. You work on a small table upstairs and have very little space. Your pencils keep rolling off it!"

She, or he, was right and this seemed to amuse them no end. I actually laughed and finally let my guard down; realising that I was dealing with an extremely professional Medium; the likes of which would put others respectfully to shame. The table they were referring to was a squat, wooden monstrosity and it moved as easily as the wind, with my pencils continuously rolling off it due to lack of space. As it happens, I now draw and paint on the kitchen table; as it offers plenty more room.

"You impersonate people!" Penny giggled. "My Guide is showing me you impersonating the Queen. They laugh at you in the world of Spirit and enjoy your imitations, especially with the voices."

Philip and I are masterful at impersonating people - right down to their body language - and my impression of the Queen always amuses family and friends. We've been doing it for years. I was fascinated at the fact that the deceased could actually see us doing this, on top of finding it highly comical. I recalled feeling somewhat uneasy at them freely being able to observe us rather as we would observe a film. Could they see everything?

"My Guide is telling me that you have a long life here on earth, this being your last incarnation."

I couldn't resist it and so interrupted her. This did not trouble Penny in the slightest.

"Can you tell me how long?" I asked. It's peculiar because I have always had a feeling - a slight feeling - that I would make old bones. "I'd really like to know."

"My Guide's telling me that he wouldn't be at all surprised if you reach your mid- eighties."

I was impressed.

"My last incarnation?" I queried. "Have I been here before?"

"You are an ancient soul," Penny informed. "Would it surprise you to know that you once lived on the continent of Atlantis, with your brother, in something called the Golden Era?"

I gasped and, again, shook my head.

"You're joking!"

"No," she reassured. "You weren't brothers then, but sisters; though not twins. Also, it was at a time when your culture embraced and interacted with beings from other worlds. Atlantis was a highly developed society and the creatures from space enhanced it with their own knowledge."

I was thunderstruck and told her so.

"So, this is my last incarnation?" I queried. "Why's that?"

"You have mastered all there is to master regarding sentiments and understanding," she explained. "Regarding past lives, it might also interest you to know that you were once a poor boy during the Egyptian Dynasty, though you were looked after by a Princess."

"Princess?"

"Yes. My Guide is showing me a scene of you with your head bowed in her lap, and she is stroking your hair," Penny informed. "You were very poor, though the Princess took pity on you, clothing and feeding you. She was a descendant of the

Royal Dynasty of Pharaohs and there was a connection between you both."

It was strange to learn this, because I have always been influenced and intrigued by the ancient Egyptian culture. As I sat there, in Penny's sitting room, with her informing me of my past lives, I began to appreciate the enormity of the entire process of our evolution; being that we apparently did not die; not in the spiritual essence, anyhow.

"Why can't we remember all this?" I frowned. "If we knew, here and now, about Heaven and our past lives, wouldn't it surely help us?"

"No it would not," she advised. "Let's say that you had a bad day tomorrow, a really bad day, but were armed with the knowledge that you are eternal and can return to a better life. Now, Ronald, you wouldn't hesitate to put a gun to your head and blow your brains out, or jump off a cliff, would you. Imagine the state of the world on a global scale if every human being alive was surely aware of this. It'd be anarchy … quite literally."

Her theory made absolute sense and sent a shiver up my spine. So, our memories of Heaven - along with our past lives - are obliterated before we agree to reincarnate and descend back down to the planet earth. I remembered thinking at the time that I must have been drunk before signing a contract - or whatever it is they do upstairs - to secure my place once again on this planet we call home.

"They have no time in the Spirit World, either," Penny continued. "They are not governed by a clock."

Ironically, there didn't seem to be enough time during the sitting to pursue more questions. However, there was one I was burning to ask. Both Philip and I have always had a fondness for the Queen ever since we were children, with the teacher telling us in junior school - all those years ago - that she could be looked upon rather like a queen bee, with her soldiers and workers all helping to maintain a colony. I asked Penny a question:

"Will Philip and I ever meet her Majesty in this life?"

Penny was not fazed.

"They're telling me that you've already met her."

She was right, though it was unofficial, and we were privileged to share a few words with Her Majesty when she visited Bedford some years back. I was, by this time, utterly convinced by the power of Spirit. Penny could not have possibly known about this incident. It was never spoken of or published.

"My Guide is telling me that you are in contact with the Crown, anyhow" she continued. "They're showing the crest over your head, along with the number 7."

That did it for me! Philip and I, without many people realising it, wrote to the Queen annually, to inform Her Majesty of our writing progress. There is absolutely no ego or intrigue to this at all, being that we look upon the Queen rather like a wise and warm Grandmother who, it must be stressed, encourages talent and which is done in private; the public having no knowledge of this whatsoever. By this time, we had indeed received 7 letters from the Crown, which are locked away in our filing cabinet; Philip and I now possess over twenty five.

"You are psychic, Ronald, like your brother," Penny enlightened. "But, it will develop when you are in your forties."

With that, the reading ended, though I wanted to ask Penny a final question before departing.

"Can you tell me what's inside the black plastic bag I brought along with me?" I asked her.

At the time, I didn't realise how impertinent this may have sounded, though she smiled at me and her eyes drifted away for a moment, once again.

"It's science fiction," she said. "Science fiction."

I opened the bag up and pulled out the painting.

"You are amazing," I told her. "And yes, it's science fiction!"

Chapter Eight

Reflection

When I returned home from the reading, I held my head in my hands and sobbed. Any doubts expressed earlier in my life as to the validity of extra-terrestrials, or that of an afterlife, were completely vanquished and I knew, deep within my heart, that they existed. I began to feel bitterness towards the churches of which I had attended in the past, along with the science teachers at school, who all blatantly denied such things and who would turn a blind eye to such questions, should they ever dare to - God forbid - raise their ugly heads.

Indeed, I do recall asking my science teacher, back at the dreaded High School, about the possibility of extra-terrestrials. The class had openly laughed at my enquiry and, to make matters worse, the teacher mocked it; reminding me that such things were not practical and that these fantastical space creatures of mine were as elusive as they were trivial to the lesson.

On the other hand, I was humbly reminded of my own trepidations concerning such things when I was younger, though I was only a juvenile with much to learn. Nevertheless, I do feel it unwise for the churches to preach such Godly matters, through the words of the Bible, only to find out that they categorically refuse the hypothesis of communicating with Spirit. They preach the good gospel, though frown upon people who have either seen Angels, or who have spoken with their loved ones by way of Mediums. This, to my mind, is a totally hypocritical approach and, on the face of it, they believe not only in a God, but also of a supernatural archangel; that of the Devil, who is quite an unpleasant chap and who awaits the wretched mortals who have wronged the Good Lord; their souls being cast out into eternal damnation by way of burning in His fiery pit of Hell.

I often wonder what the point of the Devil actually is. Wouldn't he get bored barbequing us on a daily basis? If I were him, I'd find something a little more constructive to do. I have a feeling that he was created by the churches, if only to instill fear into the masses; thus embracing God and maintaining civility and order. I have nothing against this, due to the fact that it created moralistic stability - with people recognising these virtues and becoming good citizens through such indoctrinations - though, they refuse to open their minds to more rational wonders.

Some religious cults already refer to us as 'Sinners.' However, it must be stressed that they themselves are saved from their misdeeds for embracing their beliefs ... nice to know! These people, a good many of them I believe, are accepting stagnant and dogmatic views that are becoming aged and tired. They welcome the fact of burning bushes, talking donkeys and a man that can so freely part the waves as we can run a bath - along with Adam and Eve who, Lord help them, ate an apple, with them both being denounced thereafter for impertinence - but they will categorically refuse to consider the facts of what I, and indeed a good many other souls, are currently addressing.

Recently, there have been occasions, upon expressing my views regarding the possibility of aliens and an afterlife to these so-called good Samaritans, whereby they have tried to ram the Bible down my throat; reminding me that I am referring to the Devil and that my soul will be in peril for pursuing such damnations.

"What proof do you have?" I was asked by one religious and pleasant churchgoer. "You have none."

"And neither do you," I reminded.

"The aliens you speak of are merely the trickery of the Devil," he persisted. "And, as for Spirit Communication, the Antichrist is deceiving you into believing what cannot be done."

"Hang on a minute," I said. "Didn't Jesus raise the dead?"

"We only have one shot at life," he said, ignoring my question. "The Bible states that God does not allow us second entry."

This was not enough. The person in question then persisted to try and unremittingly brainwash me into accepting the Bible as fact, and to denounce my theories, in case I should turn to the Archangel. After a vigorous debate, he told me that only one of us could be right.

"I wonder who that'd be, then?" was my curt reply. "How can I possibly challenge the church?"

They will burn my theories to the ground, yet happily force me to adopt theirs. Why? Why are they so against these topics and what is it they fear?

I would, in any case, be referred to as psychotic for daring to air my views so freely, though I will not repent my sins for addressing fascinating questions that, to my mind, need tackling. After all, don't we have the luxury of free-will?

I believe in a God, but a God that ultimately believes in me; and that is what God is. I find it hard to consider that such a beautiful deity - as magnificent as 'The One' - could punish His/Her creation through such a trivial act as questioning our genesis and universe, let alone eating an apple. They may tell me that the latter is symbolic, or a representation of man's ultimate disobedience, though I'm afraid to say that I cannot swallow it, not one little bit. It would make God appear as petty as the fabricated Devil, and that's putting it mildly.

In any event, I honoured my Grandma's wishes and read the book she had given me by the leading Medium. On that note, I have to say that I was not convinced by the author's testimony to warrant further research concerning her own, private validations.

This is the hardened trial of an amateur researcher and, I'm afraid to say, I do not accept nonsense. Whether the Medium of the book was genuine or not is beside the point, because my Grandmother had unwittingly - or wittingly - seeded an event that was to bear out, the proof of which was offered to me by a genuine Clairvoyant.

Chapter Nine

The Matron, Grandma & the Warning

Incidentally, my Grandma came to me, months after my reading with Penny, and it was in the form of a vision. Now, I must categorically stress to you that this vision was not a dream in the sense you may think, with qualified psychiatrists perhaps correcting me on the point of my subconscious mind merely concocting these scenes due to heightened wishes, longings and fears. No, it was not a dream; being coherent, stunningly visual and utterly real. If it was a dream, I have never had one before or since and it was so profound, I have not forgotten it. Also, I got the distinct impression that it was a warning, though I am still trying to decipher what it was Grandma was actually trying to tell me. I shall relay this to you accurately.

It began with me standing in a beautiful wood. This wood, I have to tell you, was of the lushest vegetation I have ever seen, with the leaves on the trees being strangely static. There was no breeze at all; no movement or sounds and I could not even discern birds, or animals within this peculiar coppice. I noticed a bright blue skyline peeking through the cracks of the dense foliage, though there was no sun.

I realized I was on a very rough, though clearly distinguishable, pathway that ran up and wound round to my left beyond the trees.

I decided to follow the pathway. Upon turning the corner, I discovered that the trail headed towards, what appeared to be, an extremely modern looking and sizable bungalow. As I advanced towards this building, I got the distinct impression that it was a type of infirmary. A generously sized porch betrayed automatic glass doors that led, from what I could make out as I progressed, to a type of reception area within. There were no cars, or ambulances parked outside the building whatsoever, as you would expect, though I knew it to be a sanatorium of some type.

As I approached the doors, they routinely parted, and I headed for the reception area which was, at the time, vacant. Beyond this, I could see a huge room that was occupied by several nurses. I could also see a sizeable woman, both tall and intimidating, standing before them and instinctively knew that she was in command; a Matron.

They had not noticed me as of yet, being distracted by talk. It was at this point when I could hear piano music emanating from an unseen part of the building; being that the room was shaped rather like an 'L.' I passed through the foyer and walked into the room.

I boldly approached the nurses, though was instantly put in my place by the Matron who quickly twirled around to give me a brazen look.

"What are you doing here?" she demanded, frowning. Her voice was gentle, though it donated an unmistakable degree of 'no-nonsense.' I clearly understood that one did not trifle with the likes of her!

"I've come to see Grandma," I replied politely, smiling at the Matron. I was rather nervous and knew that she could sense my trepidations. "Is she here?"

She gave me a hard look before responding.

"Your Grandmother is recovering here until she is fit to join the others," she informed, assertively eyeing me up and down. She hesitated for a moment, as though carefully considering my plea. "It's not standard practice for us to allow visitors, at any rate."

I just stared back at her, nervous and hopeful.

"Very well," she finally concluded, nodding; evidently sensing my anxiety. "You may have a moment with her."

The Matron then led me away from the nurses, taking the lead, and even her march signified authority as she directed me into the unseen part of the room where, upon my soul, I immediately glimpsed Grandma sitting before a piano. She was playing it, though I cannot remember the sonata. Upon seeing me, she immediately stood up and left the keyboard, hurrying over to give me a hug.

As she approached, I could see that she looked much better from the cancer, though her eyes had dark circles around them and she still looked rather frail.

"The cancer has gone," the Matron informed, turning to face me. "However, we must deal with her psychological trauma, educating her into our ways again, so that she is strong enough to continue. This place, which you come to think of as a hospital, is in actual fact a rehabilitation centre."

The Matron was undeniably aware of my thoughts!

I was staggered and knew exactly what she meant. Basically, the deceased ended up here, or in similar buildings, and I assumed that they had been devised to tackle emotional issues; gently breaking the news to the individual that they were, in actual fact, still very much alive; albeit in a spiritual dimension. I gather that - even for the most hard hearted believers - it would invariably come as something of a surprise to them, rapidly grasping the fact that they were not only immortal, but also that they must once again adopt the ways of the Spirit world and come to remember it.

A prime example, which I have been continually mulling over in my head, is that of the clock. It would pose a great challenge for us to overcome this timepiece, due to the simple fact that the next dimension - or wherever Heaven resides - does not rely on it. We are governed by it on a daily basis - from the cradle to the grave - so you can appreciate just how difficult it must be for those, who have crossed over, to break out of such habits. On top of that, there are a thousand other reasons why people end up in such sanctuaries, before they are granted leave into the Spirit World and ready to progress with their lives. Illness, trauma, dogmatic views, selfishness … the list goes on and on!

Grandma was wearing a simple negligee and, as we hugged, I had to stoop to give her a kiss on her cheek. The Matron observed our reunion in a passive mood, and it was Grandma who requested something of her this time.

"May I take my Grandson out into the forest?" she asked. "I just want to have a moment with him."

The Matron smiled back at her and nodded.

"By all means," she said and, with that, headed back towards the nurses to continue with whatever it was they were discussing.

Grandma took my hand and gave me that 'cheeky smile' she sometimes wore, leading me towards the reception area and out into the open. During this time, she said nothing, though steered me down the path from where I had come, turning right and then heading into the coppice. Along the faint trail, I saw a black metal bench positioned just before it, and she motioned for me to sit on it, with her gently parking herself beside me.

She appeared tranquil and happy, staring into my eyes with the unconditional love that always emanated from her. I was so joyful to be in her presence once again, knowing that she was - as the Matron had duly informed - recovering. The moment was priceless!

Grandma broke the silence.

"Ronnie, I am going to show you something," she said, her voice now extremely grave. "And, you must promise your Grandma that you will never forget it."

I nodded to her, though I was slightly alarmed by her anxiety. Whatever she was going to show me, I got the distinct impression that it wasn't to my benefit.

"I promise."

"It's important, Loves," she persisted, wagging that knowing finger of hers at me as though to emphasize the point. "You must never forget it."

Again, I blindly swore that I wouldn't and, with that, she did something quite extraordinary. She reached over to me and, because I had my hands resting on my lap, she placed both hers on mine, closing her eyes in the process.

The transformation was so abrupt; I had to spend a moment or two to grasp my bearings. I was home again, though outside in the back yard, and it was night; with the star spangled heavens stretching out before me. Grandma was gone and I knew, a moment later, that this is what she was illustrating; with me being present in whatever form the vision was to take.

Philip was standing beside me while I had a cigarette - never smoking indoors - and the lights in the kitchen were on. I studied the yard and noticed, to my surprise, that the huge fern tree in the back corner, and which offered a certain degree of privacy from the neighbouring houses, was gone, and that the brick wall directly before me was ragged. I got the impression that this was part of the future.

And then I heard a peculiar resonance coming from the sky. It sounded like an electronic droning, booming throughout the heavens and, upon looking up, I saw a sight that completely took my breath away. Distracted by the ruckus, Philip also observed the disruption.

"Oh, my God!" he gasped. "What the Hell are those!"

I saw, to my horror, hundreds of black triangular ships moving swiftly overhead; their size and agility mind-boggling. Many of these machines had tiny lights embedded in them which, to me, denoted portholes, as they zipped across the sky, with others shaking from side to side in a bizarre fashion that made them appear rather like irritated hornets. The noise was deafening and, upon viewing them, my instinctive nature to hide briskly kicked in, and I dived to the ground; crawling into the kitchen on all fours, with Philip in pursuit.

Those things in the sky made my skin crawl!

My first impulse was to turn off the kitchen lights. This incredible urge made sense, as I felt as though we were exposed to them - these invaders - and I reached up and flicked the switch. Having done that, I then got up and dived into the sitting room, doing the same; wondering if this assault - for that was the obvious impression I got - was being broadcast on a News Flash on TV, or whether it was occurring across the entire globe.

As it happened, the News Channel was on and the reporter, a woman dressed in a yellow blouse, was discussing a war issue occurring in another part of the world, with a televised view of tanks moving across a barren terrain behind her as she relayed the story. There was nothing, absolutely nothing, regarding the incident that had just transpired and I recalled feeling frustrated at the fact that we may very well be under attack, with the world temporarily oblivious to the impending onslaught.

And then the vision ended. That was it!

Logically, I have tried to fathom Grandma's revelation as best I can, arguing the fact that, if these ships I saw were indeed extra-terrestrial, then why invade in the future? Were they actually invading, or merely appearing to ultimately expose themselves to mankind?

Let's explore this curiosity.

If they have been here for eons, with reports of their craft loosely handed down to us through the centuries, and their soul objective is to take over our planet; wouldn't it make sense for them to have overthrown us in the past and when we were of a lesser threat? After all, we now have nuclear capability with the power to destroy and poison great continents. At present, they would fear, I believe, retaliation, should they invariably pursue such an ambitious plan; knowing only too well that the toxic effects of our weapons would ravish all hopes for their new settlement. On the other hand, they may consider our militia, to decline such an act, on the grounds of Armageddon - should we face such an assault - and challenge us until we crumble under their might and surrender. But, even so, it would require an enormous amount of effort on the alien's part, ranging from a faultless stratagem, millions of troops along with unlimited weapons and resources.

But why go to all that trouble if you're mentally and techno-logically superior to a lesser race?

They would not have to use brute force to confront us. They could, I would imagine, quite effectively create a deadly virus and introduced it into our atmosphere, thus destroying the nuisance we might pose; effortlessly seizing the planet in a silent war. They would not need to expend their own resources which is so common amongst earthly warfare and having the luxury of merely sitting back while we perish under their ingenious germ-induced assault.

Why would these extra-terrestrials want the Earth, anyway? If they are so advanced (having mastered the art of spaceflight to perfection and possessing the necessary technology) they can utilize their knowledge and build city sized ships to accommodate their species and needs; should they be without a world. And, on top of that, since they are technologically superior to us, then it surely must be within their grasp to find a habitable world and adapt it to their desires. After all, there must be hundreds of thousands of planets out there able to sustain life; our own universe being a tiny dewdrop in an ocean of galaxies.

We must consider all the possibilities, one of which alarms me and, on the face of it, raises issues and a modern-day hypothesis. Let's just say that they do not require our planet for them-selves and this conclusion is based on rational deliberation. I am certain that they could easily have crushed us decades, centuries or even eons ago, should they have had such notions of global domination. Clearly, they do not.

Then why are they here? Well, that leaves a few options open for debate, though I am inclined to believe just one. They require us, or need us for something. If you think about it, this assumption is quite reasonable and which we shall explore later in the book.

Incidentally, the huge fern at the back of our yard was removed some years after the vision (which I had eleven years ago) and so it remains to be seen if this event will eventually occur; if it is to be believed that my Grandmother was offering me an insight into the arrival of an extra-terrestrial force.

Chapter Ten

The Kempston Spiritualist Church

I believe we, as human beings, have an insatiable lust for proof based on our own personal exploits. Even though I had seen Penny and was offered incredible evidence of life after death - along with learning that I was an old soul who had incarnated centuries ago - I still wanted further verification.

Philip and I discovered a Spiritualist Church along the road from where we lived, which conducted clairvoyant demonstrations and so, after briefly enquiring when the services were held, we decided to pay a visit.

The church was basically a hall within a modern building, with us having to climb a flight of stairs - or alternatively use the lift - to reach it. Upon rounding the designated level, we could hear many voices coming from the hall and knew that this was where the services were conducted.

It was spacious and, from what we could tell, quite crowded too; with people, both standing and seated, chatting before the proceedings got underway at 7.30pm. Philip and I didn't know anyone present, though they made us feel extremely welcome as we appeared through the doorway; all smiling and informing us that there were free refreshments available during the interval. We decided to take a seat in the back row of the room, feeling moderately comfortable being out of eyeshot of the Medium who, as it happened, was seated at the front behind a table, along with the chairman who was talking with her.

We didn't even know who the Medium was; being a brown-haired woman in her late thirties and, as the chairman rose to introduce her to the group, we sat alert and expectant; wondering how it was she would bring the deceased through. Would it be like Penny? Did she have a Spirit Guide, too?

Having thanked the Medium for coming, the chairman then sat himself down as she proceeded to explain how she communicated with the Other Side. Basically, it was identical to Penny's technique; summoning her own Spirit Guide who acted as mediator between our two worlds. Upon initiating her clairvoyance, she then focused her attention on the back row; briskly pointing at both me and Philip.

"There's a lovely rainbow connecting you both at the back," she said, emphasising the fact by wagging her finger from side-to-side. Heads briskly turned in the congregation to view, if they could, the identical newcomers. "Your Grandma's here, boys, and she died of cancer."

Philip thanked her and her Spirit Guide for the kind compliment, along with acknowledging the fact that our Grandmother had indeed died from the dreadful disease.

"Your Grandma's standing before a man who died drowning ... it was tragic," she continued, unable to see us suitably for the sea of heads in her way. "He was in the Navy."

I recalled turning to face Philip, my eyes wide at the accuracy of the information she was channelling from her Guide.

"You both have a birthday coming up, because your Grandma's showing me her whisking ingredients together in a ceramic bowl. She's also singing."

Again, Philip acknowledged that our birthday was but a few weeks away and, being that Grandma loved to cook, she always used the traditional, brown ceramic bowl to whip up her rock cakes and bread puddings, to name but a few.

"Now, your Grandma's telling me that this is your last incarnation, as you are old souls," she continued. "She's showing me you tying up your shoelaces, as an example of you securing all the loose ends, before you return home to the world of spirit. She's also showing me intricate tapestry, or fine drawings, that you enjoy doing. There is gold coming down over you too and this is connected with the tapestry. Do you understand this?"

"Yes," I nodded. "The gold may be a reward?"

"I can only relay what they're showing me," she acknowledged. "Grandma will wait for you and your family and see you into the light."

It was on that note that our reading ended, and she proceeded to move on to another person seated ahead of us; bringing through the evidence thick and fast. She was, I agreed with Philip, simply amazing. The fact that we had never seen her before in our lives, or knew anyone in the entire congregation for that matter, was unshakable proof that she was indeed communicating with a dimension that not only eluded us, but one which currently challenges the dull views of debunkers who still, to this day, purport to believe that these gifted individuals are merely offering so-called 'cold readings' to the masses; that of fooling the sitter into believing they are in contact with a loved one by analysing his/her hairstyle, clothes, facial expression, body language - that sort of thing - and to cleverly compile all this evidence together, thus forming a fitting picture of the individual and qualifying as a so-called Medium.

I would happily agree with them - personally embracing this in favour of a more plausible explanation, being the rational minded person that I am - were it not for the simple fact that the Medium could not even see us. And, I have to tell you, she was fast!

Of course, there are charlatans out there, ready and waiting to fool a sitter into believing that they can actually channel the deceased through by using just such a process, and this fact alone gives debunkers - yet again - ammunition to fire at the genuine types who are, more than not, persecuted for practising this unorthodox, yet highly fascinating enigma.

As it happened, Philip and I visited the church on many more occasions, whereby Grandma was waiting to communicate; humourously jumping the queue to be first in line, just to get her message across to us once again. When the fourth Medium brought her through from spirit, the congregation actually laughed as she cheekily stole the limelight. However, Philip and I categorically knew that she was using it to her advantage, mustering every means at her disposal to drum the message into our heads that she was alive and well; albeit in another dimension.

Grandma never returned after that and we knew, even back then, that she had more important things to deal with; namely her life. We were, in any event, fortunate to receive her, along with the many relatives and friends who communicated with us thereafter; grateful for their love and kind memories. It's funny because, having learnt so much about this subject from my brother - who is a professional working Medium himself - I find it quite incredible to discover just how insensitive some people can actually be during a reading.

"Why can't David come through?" is an example of this. "I want David."

You just can't demand their presence at the drop of a hat because they, like us, are doing their own things. It's rather like me making a telephone call to America - to an old friend - only to find out that he's in Alaska with his mates. We are so indoctrinated into believing that Heaven can and must simply stand still for us - when in the presence of a Medium - and that anyone and everyone present in it are at our beck and call. This would denote a degree of ignorance on our part, with the sitter appearing aloof as to why the Medium cannot channel so-and-so through. One or two sitters, I know from Philip, have arrived at our house with a measure of snobbishness about them during their readings; leisurely toying with the process and having the audacity to demand afterwards why Aunty Nora came through, instead of, "that handsome old devil I knew back in my 40's and who perished in a car crash." Perhaps the handsome old devil had better sense in steering clear of Lady Muck!

Some people will not swallow this, debating that, since their loved ones are in the world of Spirit, then surely they must be able to whip their ethereal-selves over to the Medium for a natter. To adopt such a thought is selfish and impertinent. Would you like to talk to someone here who - let's just say - double-crossed you or treated you unfairly? Unless you have sorted out your differences, or succumbed to your irritation, then the answer must surely be, 'No.' Why then should it be any different in the Spirit world? Just because they've moved on to a higher form of expression, doesn't mean to say they've swallowed 'A Cheerful Pill' which offers them nothing but unconditional love to every Tom, Dick and Harry that should command their presence.

Philip and I, along with the family, never told Granddad King about us visiting Mediums and receiving messages from Grandma, just in case he scolded us for tampering with the unknown; especially after the incident with the book. As a matter of fact, we weren't entirely sure how he'd react, so we kept it quiet.

In any event, Granddad would have had more than a fit, if he knew what Philip and I did, following the church services, and would have definitely reprimanded us on the grounds of stupidity because, under my clear instructions, we both decided to defy his supernatural trepidations and to explore the world of the Ouija Board.

Chapter Eleven

The Ouija Board

The Ouija Board did not come about purely on the impulse of inquisitiveness; rather, the idea was planted in my head by an urgency I cannot explain. Philip and I were at home one evening, with our dear friend and artist, Susan, and were discussing the Mediums we had seen; furnishing her with the evidence they had supplied to us and marvelling at the incredible nature of it. It was at this point that I suggested we try a private method of contact by using just such a device.

We did not, at the time, possess an Ouija Board - clearly never having any such notion to use one - though I quickly began to cut up small pieces of paper, with Philip writing out the letters of the alphabet on each one, and then accordingly arranging them in a circular fashion around the kitchen table. The planchette, we decided, would be a small glass tumbler, which I commandeered from the cabinet, and which moved quite smoothly on the polished wood.

Having set up the table, Philip and I decided to experiment first; moving the tumbler across to each and every letter - with us both resting a finger gently on its base - to see how it fared. There was a slight problem; we inadvertently shifted the letters with our sleeves as we moved the glass, messing up the lower circle. Due to lack of time, decided that - if it should work - then we would make a proper board out of wood, with the letters inscribed on it. We would just have to manage for the time being.

Now, I must firmly stress to you, before I continue, that it is not wise to fool around with a Ouija Board, unless you have nothing but the best of intentions at heart and do not abuse it. Like anything else, if you respect it, it will invariably respect you. They are not toys!

We decided that we were ready to attempt communication with whomever it was we should call in the Spirit world, with Susan perched at one end of the table; pen and paper at the ready, to transcribe the letters which would hopefully form coherent sentences. An interesting point we discovered upon making contact - and which should be addressed at this point - was the fact of us having missed a designated 'Space Bar' to indicate the breaking of a word; though the planchette cleverly circled the centre of the table to emphasise this point quite beautifully when we had established a suitable link.

We opened with a respectful prayer, asking the Spirit world to offer us protection against any menacing articles that should happen to infiltrate our session; guarding us from - what Philip now terms as - 'The Lower Entities' and ensuring that we were shielded before addressing the Other Side. Through research, it has come to our attention that such beings do exist and dwell on a lower astral plane from those in the Spirit World; being murderers, rapists, child molesters, to name but a few.

Our protection prayer became a humourous catchphrase used in the brilliant *Star Trek* episodes, created by Gene Roddenberry, and which we recited quite frequently during our sessions; announcing; "Shields Up!" In any event, since the people on the Other Side have humour - a quality that still baffles many today - we decided to share it with them; albeit in an appropriate manner.

The pessimistic opening sentence, and which has been so heavily used on TV and films, by asking, "is anyone there?" is utter twaddle. This is neither humourous nor factual, placing the entire session in a negative light and which effectively ridicules it. Our first communication with them was not by announcing such a degrading line, but by way of saying absolutely nothing.

Philip and I held our fingers on the glass, concentrating on it, and we emptied our minds of any trivial thoughts that might be roaming around. After a while, I could feel my finger becoming slightly warm and Philip confirmed this too. Susan watched from across the table in bemused silence as the glass, very slowly, began to edge its way towards the letter 'Y.'

Now, you may very well think that one of us was unceremoniously influencing the tumbler by forcing it in the direction we sought. This was not the case; we ourselves wanting proof and being driven, as usual, by a no-nonsense code of conduct. If it worked, it worked. If it didn't ... we'd simply terminate the experiment.

Eventually, it spelt the word 'YES,' followed by the glass moving into the centre of the table, whereby it twirled about. After that, it invited us to, "ASK," with the glass, once again, repeating its coil pattern which we quickly discerned as being an invisible space-bar.

"Who are we talking to?" Philip asked. "Can you identify yourself?"

Once again, the glass moved to form a name and this, as it turned out, was a friend of Philip's who had sadly died of cancer. We'll call him Gary.

"How are you, Gary?" Philip asked.

"Fine - it's everything you said it would be, and more."

Philip, by this time, was developing rather quickly with his psychic training, and had explained to Gary, (before he passed away), that we did not merely expire; educating him on the survival of human consciousness after we die.

I interrupted the session.

"We need proof that we are actually communicating with you, Gary," I boldly informed. "I'd like to try something."

The glass remained inactive on the board as I turned to face Susan.

"Susan, write something down on a piece of paper and don't reveal it to us," I advised. "If you wish, leave the room and think up a word, or name ... anything, but keep it to yourself. We'll ask Gary what it is."

Susan duly complied, leaving the room and returning a moment later. She had written something down on a piece of paper, which was now folded up in her pocket. I then readdressed the board.

"Gary, can you please tell us what it is Susan has written?"

There was no response.

"Gary, we need to know."

The glass began to move again. It spelt, "Trickery."

"No, we are not trying to trick you," I curtly informed. "If you can look at it from our perspective, and if you were in our position, you'd completely understand why we are kindly asking this of you. Please, Gary ... it would validate the experiment and guarantee us peace of mind."

After a few minutes, the glass began to move again; this time a little faster. I couldn't help but wonder whether it was out of frustration - or a newfound sense of urgency - simply to prove a point. After all, Gary and I weren't close, due to the fact that he selected his friends very carefully. I did not, I'm afraid to say, wholly qualify.

It read, "D,A,R,T,H - M,A,U,L."

Because Gary loved the 'Star Wars' films created by George Lucas, he chose the name of one of the characters featuring in the first of the new trilogy and which had just been screened at the cinema. Philip and I were hopeful, though I couldn't help but feel a little sceptical, because the name itself - and coming from Spirit - seemed too bizarre to verify such a test. If he was wrong, I had decided - there and then - to terminate the experiment; knowing that the unreliable information could not possibly assist us and which would, in any case, throw the entire process into question.

Susan briskly stood up and appeared surprised, removing the sheet of paper from her trouser pocket. I shall never forget that moment because, as she unfolded it, she did not utter a single word. She merely showed it to us. In bold letters, it read:

'DARTH MAUL.'

We knew, there and then, that we were dealing with a force beyond our wildest dreams and, to cheekily prove a point, the glass began to move once again as Gary revelled in the moment.

"Are you happy now, Ronald?"

"Yes," I said. "I am. Thank you, Gary."

We then began to contact Gary on a regular basis, requesting information from him regarding the Spirit world and its environment. These gatherings were referred to as 'Board Meetings' and we had two or three of them a week, with Susan kindly transcribing the information for us. We fondly nicknamed the Ouija Board as 'Our Psychic Typewriter,' being that it was slow and arduous, though it worked beautifully and Gary, at the time, proved to be an invaluable source of information regarding 'the other side.'

From the data we amassed from him, it became quite evident to us that Gary resided in his own personal world; swimming, sunbathing, relaxing etc and that this realm was rather like a tropical island. We soon learnt that it was a temporary abode and that he did not - so it seemed - require the rehabilitation centre to adjust; preferring his own solitude to overcome the pain and anguish of dying so soon while on Earth. Interestingly, I have often heard reports of people who, after having a brief brush with death, were transported to varied lands; suggesting that the geography of the Spirit world may not be entirely static. Could it be possible that the phrase we have charmingly coined 'mind over matter' may apply here and that the souls residing in this dimension are based in their own and preferred establishments; with no constraints that so commonly plague our own?

After a good half year, we never heard from Gary again, though Philip's own Spirit Guide, Wolfsong, took over the sessions; providing many insights into our lives and those of the so-called deceased that are now governed by new laws of science which would invariably turn our own rational wisdom upside-down.

These sessions also became of interest to Penny who, having requested the progress of Philip's psychic training, befriended us and our family and who, as it turned out, made regular visits to our house. This led to many more incredible discoveries, one of which I shall relay to you in the next chapter because, as it turned out, she advised 'Past-Life Regression.' I was shortly to discover some startling facts that were extremely visual regarding my own history; one of which involved an extra-terrestrial force and which inspired me not only write to about it, but to also illustrate them and their technology, which I clearly discerned through this extraordinary voyage of my former self.

Chapter Twelve

Past Life Regression

Having already demonstrated her incredible gift as a Medium, it was at one of our weekly meetings, at our house, when Penny suggested performing Past Life Regression on me. I was excited at the time, and happily agreed, with us arranging a suitable date for the occasion.

By this time, I was growing increasingly curious about my own past lives - on the premise that we reincarnated on a regular basis - and from what little I had gleaned about Atlantis. Because I believe our memories of the past are whitewashed to prevent problems from arising (as documented earlier) I was overcome with a deep sense of inquisitiveness as to what this aged old empire actually looked like in its heyday. Perhaps it took on the form of Rome; or the ancient pyramids of Giza! Whatever the outcome, I was enthralled at having Penny kindly spare her time in order to seek out my own historical secrets that were conveniently locked away in some elusive part of my mind.

The day arrived and Penny came at around midday. We had tea and chatted for a while, before retiring to the sitting-room where the experiment was to be conducted; I call it an experiment because we were, at this stage, unsure if it would work on me or not. Besides, she informed me that not every case was successful and that the procedure was a delicate and lengthy one. I was certainly up for the challenge.

Penny was seated before me and I sat in a comfortable armchair, relaxing, as she produced a notebook and pen.

Strangely, I was not apprehensive.

"I'd like to know what phobias you have before we start," she asked, opening her book with pen poised on a page. "Also, what colours are you attracted to?"

I told her that I disliked spiders and heights and that my favourite colours were blue, silver, black and gold.

"Do you have any issues with people here, ranging from the past to the present?"

I told her that I didn't, discounting trivial matters that could not, to my mind, represent any concerns for what we were about to attempt.

A whole host of questions were put forward (most of which I cannot, for the life of me, remember) until Penny was satisfied that she had recorded as much information as possible. I gathered she was to use this data as a comparison-chart on the off chance that the experiment succeeded.

"Okay, we'll begin," she smiled. "I want you to relax and close your eyes. Empty your mind of any thoughts. Shortly, I shall begin hypnosis and send you into a semiconscious state."

I conjured a large blackboard within my mind and stared back at its dark canvas; able to dispel any thoughts that might linger or intrude as I focused on it. It seemed to work rather well. To try and quieten the mind is a difficult challenge in itself, though the soothing atmosphere and expert guidance was enough to convince me that it could be done. In any event, I was aware that I would undoubtedly have to view any promising and historical episodes as pictures formed within my mind, so the canvas was an ideal choice.

Penny then began to count down and, as she did so, I actually felt at peace; slowly drifting into a cocooned state of tranquillity that intensified as the numbers decreased.

"Any natural or external noises will not disturb the session," she continued. "You shall be at peace during the regression and know that nothing can harm you whatsoever."

I drifted deeper and deeper, feeling my entire body relaxing as she succeeded in transporting me into a semiconscious state. Even my hands, nimbly resting on my thighs, felt light and ethereal, and the remote humdrum sounds of the occasional passing cars - penetrating the double glazing - softened and died as I, for the first time in my life, let go of all trepidations. The world as I knew it temporarily expired, dissolving into oblivion as I concentrated on Penny's voice; calmly staring into the dark and inactive blackboard ahead of me.

"I now want you to go back in time, back to your previous lives on this world." Penny quietly instructed. "I want you to record as many of them as you can and to remember them when I recall you back to your present incarnation."

Her words sounded somewhat distant as I casually absorbed them. I strangely felt as though I was standing on the brink of a great and dubious abyss, though I bore in mind her words that no harm would come to me during the session.

A considerable amount of time passed as I stared back at the black canvas, when I could see nothing on it whatsoever. I then decided to which liberate myself of any doubts by taking a step into the great abyss had no sound, form or colour. I did not fall, as you would expect, but rather; was immediately transported into a world of broken scarlet and white. It took a moment for me to realise that this was a cloud formation and that it was moving at an implausible speed.

I watched as this effect continued. After a while, the clouds began to fade and I saw, for the first time during the session, an image on my blackboard. This intensified and, rather like a motion picture, I watched in absolute awe as I saw myself standing before the great pyramids of Giza that were, I must stress, incomplete. This film was accompanied by a sort-of knowing - a sensation that told me who I was and where I was - though it was mute in every respect.

I was a scrawny, bronzed, ancient looking man and I knew that I was the equivalent of a Councillor (or something of that kind) for the Royal Household. The pyramids were in the process of being constructed. I was present to oversee a new piece being hoisted up, ready to be positioned within a huge square hole expertly dug in the ground before me; and of which was part of the great pyramid of Cheops, the largest of the three.

I wore a thin top, and was modestly covered below, and I do recall wearing sandals of some type. The sand around me was insufferable due to the heat and I gathered that it must have been around midday, or thereafter. Flanking me, a multitude of similarly dressed dignitaries watched the manoeuvre with keen deliberation; myself recording the event with the later intent of briefing the reigning Pharaoh of the time. It must, I gathered, have been an important occasion - or a crucial one - because the feeling I was experiencing was a mixture of optimism and anxiety. I could not recall what exactly it was the architects were essentially doing.

I moved closer to the pit to gain a better view, knowing that the colossal limestone blocks suspended above my head were, at that point, being lowered ... though something went terribly wrong!

I recalled a great commotion coming from behind. Even though I have already explained to you that the entire experience was muted, I acquired this through pure sensation and I spun around, observing the dignified congregation behind me pointing up in alarm. I then turned back to look up and noticed, to my immediate horror, the gigantic blocks falling; the cradle - or whatever it was they used to lower them - having cleanly shattered.

It was over in an instant. Because I was bordering on the edge of the pit, one of the blocks struck me and I fell headlong with it, plunging into the deep crevice (undoubtedly dead at that point) with the rest of them tumbling in after me; sand and debris temporarily choking and blinding the region in a plume of catastrophe and death. It was then when the broken clouds of scarlet and white returned, passing over me as I headed for another incarnation.

This time, I was in the capital city of Rome, during the height of a ruthless, yet effective, sovereignty; that of the Roman Empire. I was within the major coliseum in Italy - the largest ever constructed - and was, once again, in peril.

The elliptical amphitheatre, mainly used for gladiatorial games, plays and executions was, at this moment in time, being utilized as a bloodbath; much to the amusement and joy of its spectators who roared and jeered while seated in a tiered arrangement within the colossal building. I was, upon viewing myself, a boy of around fourteen or fifteen years of age; meagrely dressed in shoddy garments and running within the centre of the arena. It was evident to me, as I watched the scenario unfold, that I - along with many others - was being used for sport by the ambitious gladiators. This game, I knew, was performed to instill hatred into the conformed masses for allowing my kind - whatever religion I embraced - to walk the Earth, with the killings ultimately fuelling their sense of pride in the Roman empire; an empire which sought to sterilize anything and everything that did not conform to its Head of State.

The gladiators, with their impressive amour and imposing headgear, were energetically pursuing us within the coliseum; their swords slashing and digging as they caught men, women and children off guard. Others hunted in chariots drawn by white stallions, efficiently decapitating their rivals, while the horses charged over the slain, with the bodies being trampled into the bloodied and dusty sand that covered the ground.

I was utterly frantic and knew, within my heart, that I was doomed. People were falling all around me; with the hapless victims possessing nothing with which to defend themselves.

I suddenly noticed a passing chariot in close proximity and immediately lunged for it, grasping the rear as it pursued a man; trying as best I could to clamber up and apprehend the warrior steering it. The adrenaline was pumping throughout my body and I was determined, against all the odds, to survive the ordeal. But, as I raised myself up behind the unremitting gladiator, I saw another swooping in on me; his sword fully drawn. He easily ploughed it into my back, expertly driving the blade through to my heart and impaling me; breaching the lower part of my chest. I instantly collapsed and fell behind the chariot as it trundled forth, with the bloodied sword being extracted by the proud warrior. It was at this point when the broken scarlet and white clouds returned, progressively taking me from this era and into yet another.

The images I saw did not disturb me. I was spellbound at the clarity of them. There was, as of yet, no Atlantis to be seen, though I was composedly intrigued to learn more of what I had experienced in past lives. This, I assure you, was not conjured from a subconscious willingness to see what I saw, nor was it based on fanciful dreams ... no, the images were startling and coherent and I knew enough to realize that I was actually looking at myself centuries ago.

And yet, I was experiencing death ... nothing but death!

Once again, the clouds diminished and I saw a new scene. This time, I was a Roman soldier, clad in uniform, and came to realize that I, along with my fellow warriors, was in the middle of a battle.

Mounted ally horses were charging past me in the midst of confusion and anger; the enemy having clashed with our battalion upon us markedly breaching their territory in an effort, no doubt, to expand the Roman empire. I saw men on both sides fall and the weapons which our foes possessed were equally inventive and deadly.

I, along with my division, was driving back a group of antagonists who, at this time, had dismounted their own horses; driven by a murderous willingness to polish us off. One of them, I noticed, wielded an unpleasant looking ball connected to a chain, and which had exaggerated spikes poking out of it at every angle. He was swinging it around with such ferocity that I felt sure he disregarded his own life; favouring exposure from his mount to skillfully brandish the brutal weapon in a lethal act of vengeance. Perhaps I had killed his brother, or a relative of his, because it was beginning to feel personal as he approached me. A few of his men followed suite, all appearing equally intimidating.

They expertly downed my men, stabbing and clubbing them to death; leaving me vulnerable. The confusion around me was perplexing as the war grotesquely unfolded; though I concentrated on the advancing enemy now poised to strike. As they targeted me, I daringly flashed by sword at them; waving it around in an effort to intimidate and discourage any further thought of encroachment. However, my tactic failed and, before I knew it, two of them were upon me; briskly knocking me to the ground with my back pressed against the dirt. I was lying exposed before them, having been swiftly disarmed.

The one brandishing the metal ball then did something quite loutish, spinning the lethal contraption around so fast that it became a blur of silver. With proficient accuracy, he bought it down to my covered private parts, and, as it slammed into them, I saw a gush of blood spurt up, which stained some of the men. I died from the shock and injury; left to rot along with the others as our rivals continued with their campaign in driving the Roman Legion back to its ruthless Emperor.

And then, the familiar clouds returned, signifying the end of another era. I was, by this time, wondering why I was experiencing nothing but death, rather than seeing a golden time of enlightenment and prosperity in whatever land or form it took. Nonetheless, the final viewing did not portray morbid scenes of swift terminations because, unbeknown to me, I was shortly to become utterly shell-shocked at what I beheld; in a land that was as beautiful as it was monumental.

The last incarnation I saw was one which coincidently held appeal to me because, as it began to unfold, I discovered I was part of the Mayan civilization in Chichén Itzá, located in the northern centre of the Yucatán Peninsula, Mexico. Having recently researched this incredible and architectural wonderment, I have uncovered certain elements that may corroborate what I witnessed.

Incidentally, my Mother has visited Chichén Itzá and, when she returned, she told me about this culture's customs, their technological advancements as well as the sacrifices they made to the Gods. These were applied upon winning games. Possibly games equivalent to our modern day Olympics.

In this vision, I was a bronzed man with jet-black hair and my physique was impressive. From the vantage point I had I was able to observe myself, I was leaning on a stone banister with a woman standing to my right; being on a hill or some type of elevated structure. She had long dark locks and was staring out at the impressive scenery; surveying the immense

THE MAYAN REPTILIAN GODS

DISEMBARKING THEIR SHIP AT CHICHÉN ITZÁ TO BE GREETED
BY THE MAYAN DIGNITARIES

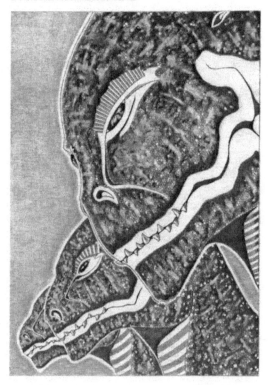

buildings of our civilization that peeked above a dense and expansive jungle. This woman, I knew with certainty, was Philip. Whether we were brother and sister, or husband and wife, I have no idea and, as much as the latter may disturb you, we must carefully appreciate the fact that, at the time, it would not have mattered in the slightest; being that we have evidently incarnated together on numerous occasions.

The sky was a deep blue, with a modicum of cloud, and I could seen the distant silhouettes of tropical birds, occasionally soaring above the dense trees as they went to-and-fro about their business.

I was expectant and knew that we had gathered there for a reason.

And then I saw why. Something colossal was descending from the sky. Upon viewing it, I had the feeling it was a frequent visitor.

On the mound, or whatever it was we were standing on, we both observed a gigantic, squat, silver, spider-like ship that sophisticatedly dropped into the Mayan settlement. It was, I have to tell you, the most peculiar looking thing I have ever seen and I was aware, upon viewing it, that it was heading towards a special court; just beyond the fringe of the colony and which had been especially constructed for it. I also knew, along with my spouse, that the Gods had once again returned to be welcomed by our society.

As it descended, disappearing behind the trees, I felt an urge to turn and observe my left wrist. I was wearing a golden device that resembled a small, circular screen and instinctively knew that it was not part of my own technology; but that of the visiting Gods. I was also aware that it was some type of communication device which the aliens utilized. However, although it was inactive, I keenly studied it.

THE MAYAN SPACECRAFT

Effectively coming into landing upon a portion of the
Mayan settlement known to me as the 'Courtyard.'

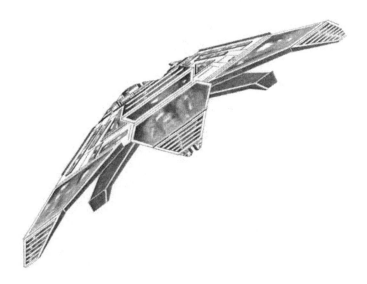

The ship was settling itself on the ground, with a welcoming
committee gathering to greet the masters of it; their presence
signifying either a break from their own headquarters, or
additional research based on the lesser colony they
categorically governed. I then had a flash of them (their faces
to be exact) and what I saw actually caused me to wince.

Serpents! Or, to adopt a more modern-day expression,
reptiles! Their countenance was striking and one which has
remained firmly fixed in my mind ever since. I have, at any
rate, illustrated them, along with aspects of their technology,
for you to view, and I hope that you can get a feel for what I
actually observed.

Now, the most interesting point here is that, back then, I had absolutely no knowledge of the Mayan civilization. In effect, I knew nothing about them. Imagine my surprise at finding, after recording the results of the experiment, that they actually worshipped the serpent and, further more, had it cast into their very own culture by way of carvings and sculptures. Indeed, the Temple of Kukulcan portrays stone snakes at its base - a representation of their God - the feathered serpent. And, upon the two equinoxes, an impressive show of light and shadow is exhibited on the staircase of this shrine, casting an illusion and giving the semblance of these reptilian depictions essentially descending from the top to the bottom. The technology of this edifice is astounding!

Was this an ethereal God they bestowed adulation? I don't think so, though the Mayan community - along with a whole host of archaeologists and scholars - may think differently. I am a mere upstart with no archaeological experience whatsoever and contest their established values; and the community's ability to construct buildings that can reverberate sound waves in such a precise manner - along with having an astronomy with them being acquainted with the solar system - in favour of extra-terrestrial intervention which may well have aided their technological know-how.

I have recorded this event to contest their theory and to perhaps open their eyes to the fact that the Mayans may indeed have had contact with a race of creatures from another world, or dimension. After all, wouldn't we ourselves - at this time - bestow gracious wonderment upon an advanced civilization visiting us? Wouldn't we look upon them as Gods for what they had achieved and for what they could ultimately teach us?

Were the serpentine Gods physically in attendance with the Mayan race; savouring the peculiar customs that endeared them to this tribe and one which they possibly rewarded? No doubt, the aliens would - upon their original arrival - have already studied them, both psychologically and biologically; or knew of their genesis. That being the case, what wonders did they bestow upon these people to secure holy amnesty for the idols they purported to be? What price did the Mayans have to pay in exchange for the skills they attained? There is, after all, an old saying; "You don't get something for nothing."

Moving on a little, I have a theory regarding these possible overlords - the Reptilians - and the shadowy Grays. I believe that the former are ancient, with the latter having been created by them to act as servants. Might it also be possible - dare I say - to speculate that we ourselves are nothing more than byproducts of these reptilian gods, with them having modified our species by way of genetic manipulation; having used the original apelike descendant of Earth to carry tailored embryos which eventually gave rise to our species? This new race, the serpents knew, would supersede the intellectually-starved primeval kind that did not stand a chance - regardless of Darwin's theory - and which has, as beautifully orchestrated, become the forerunners of academic supremacy.

Perhaps we ourselves were an experiment; one which has either pleased the reptiles, or damaged their tactics by way of us having eventually separated from the revised kin, to govern alternative lands; thus creating division and subsequent alienation from each another. Flags of distinction, they may well argue (being that they are still very much in existence) play a terrible path in personal domination, with suspicion and subsequent warfare resulting from one faction trying to outwit the other in every conceivable way.

Perhaps the Mayans, in their innocence, knew that they (and their descendants) had been modified by the aliens; understanding their place before these superior overlords.

Are they secretly observing us at this very moment, waiting to extend their hand, to the diligent champions of science and technology, once the supreme faction of humanity has finally proved its worth? And, to what end? Will they reveal themselves to their victors, announcing that they are, to every degree, the *bona fide* Fathers; having tailored them to perfect, like the Grays, a slave-race?

This being the case, I suspect that they will not make themselves known as of yet; hiding behind the veils of sinister establishments who are gullible enough to form a coalition with them; if only for personal gain. We have, as they may well observe, embraced dogmatic views; religion being the crux and which has brainwashed us into believing that there can only be one true God; depending on our consecrated virtues. To be informed that we ourselves were created by a master race would undoubtedly throw the spanner into the works; thus shattering a faith that has been instilled into us for thousands of years. It would, I believe, create anarchy on an unprecedented scale.

The serpents would first need to smash this faith very carefully and coherently, and I believe that the process is already in motion. We are, after all, being forced into a dictatorship; regardless of how subtle it may seem at present. The reptilians are applying this through the naïve people, who, like the Mayans, stoop to their demands, and our world is becoming a very cold, undisciplined, electronically-applied Aladdin's Cave which they relish ...and of which they are slowly and coherently gaining control of.

To steer society towards a personal goal, one must first starve it of its civil rights.

So why can't there be two Gods - or three? Why are we so transfixed on the one? Yes, to be rational, the one is the all which encompasses the mass, though we must not forget our own place in the universe. We are not, I have to reiterate, masters of it; nor will we ever be and, as sour as this fact may seem, we must accept it.

After all, we still know very little about our own solar system, let alone explain how the entire universe began, or whether there is an edge to it, or if it is infinite for that matter. And, if it is endless, what exactly is infinity? We can easily define it as a word, but to understand it; well, that takes some beating. We are told that the 'big bang' occurred, which shaped matter and the like, but what caused the 'big bang' and what was there before that? What exactly is space and what are we in if it is to be believed there is a border ... which there must be, for one simple and logical observation:

Whether the cosmos is expanding or contracting, it categorically justifies a basis having boundaries; the mass being driven by a force that has been thrust out from a distant core. To expand would validate birth (on an unprecedented scale) and to contract would denote death; however many trillions of Earth years it will take for us - along with our entire neighbours - to be sucked back up into the one ... perhaps to explode once again and revise life, if the 'big bang' theory is to be believed.

Also, how is it that planet Earth, which weighs billions of tons, can effortlessly hang in the great expanse - appearing as light as a feather - along with her neighbours? Perhaps it is relative to the gravitational pull of each encompassing the sun; but the speed is sluggish in comparison and which cannot maintain the perfected balance required to keep it, and them, from falling.

Space itself, the very fabric that webs entire solar systems and the cosmos together, may very well hold an interesting secret! After all, it does not turn like the worlds we have catalogued and so gravity is nonplus ... but a nonplus enigma that can support not only the tiniest of moons, but those of the largest of stars, is utterly startling.

To my mind, and on reflection, space is rather like an ocean. From a feather to a gargantuan ship, our aquatic mass can support all weight (depending on the bulk, of course) and if not steered, items or vessels are carried off by currents. Sometimes, whirlpools occur; so could these minute earthly incidents hold a likeness to the more powerful attributes of the cosmos; namely the fact that it can support our moons, planets and stars; along with giving rise to destructive anomalies (such as black holes) that tear its framework up, just as whirlpools disturb the waters of our world. To that end, it would appear that even our celestial and seemingly infinite blackness suffers from raging storms and prevailing destruction; an outcome that proves that it must have some kind of structure to it that we ourselves, as of yet, cannot grasp.

It is sensible to assume that we share a common denominator with the heavens.

To state and publish matter-of-fact accounts relating to the 'big bang' theory is, to my mind, inconsistent; considering we hardly understand the laws of our great cosmos and how it exactly began. After all, its genesis was not witnessed. Scholars tell us that they can prove this theory by using simulations and other exotic models, though these are based purely on human numerical systems which the universe may not complement.

I am in no way denouncing the brilliant scientists and astronomers of our world. In fact, I give them humble credence in their efforts to understand our origins, though this fact - which they have brazenly announced - simply cannot be proved and I personally believe that the answer may lie in the atom itself. After all, if you look at it through diagrams, it does seem to resemble a solar system in itself; the nucleus being the Sun, and the surrounding electrons representing the numerous planets, with them orbiting it, rather like we orbit our own star. Everything is composed of the atom and so we should, if you like, be referred to as 'Star Children;' upon observing this blueprint that has unquestionably been derived from the Universe's own humble material.

Returning to the past life regression, I concluded that it was enough to persuade me to embrace it with credence, knowing

THE WRIST-DISC

Basic illustration of Reptilian technology. The golden wrist-disc was a communication device which the extra-terrestrials entrusted to those suited for consultation.

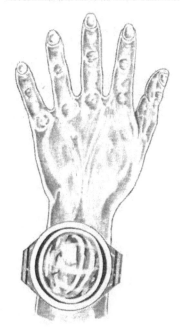

fully that I could not have possibly drummed such scenes from the far corners of my mind; no matter what psychologist would predictably conclude.

After the session, Penny absorbed the details and told me to reflect on them - which I did - and then suggested something quite bizarre.

"You are psychic yourself," she told me. "But, it will progress when you reach your forties. In the meantime, I want you to try something that I believe you can do. The gift you have at writing and drawing may be beneficial to you. Have you ever heard of, Automatic Writing?"

I told her that I had, though I was dubious. In effect, I would have to consciously blank my mind and trust in my own guide - who I did not know and who is, to be honest, a complete stranger to me - and to let him or her use me as a scribing instrument, based on questions I would put forward.

I was excited about this new experiment and told Penny that I would give it a try, if only to see if I could attain results.

Chapter Thirteen

Automatic Writing

A few months later, I attempted automatic writing; preferring the comfort of an armchair in the sitting room, with a textbook and pen at the ready. I chose to try the experiment in the evening, with the house being empty and quiet. It was also at a time when I felt quite relaxed, with little or no worries to hinder the trial.

I closed my eyes and asked for my nameless and faceless guide to join me. I have not, to this day, made a formal acquaintance with him/her; but this entity remains loyal at all times and who I talk to on a regular basis when faced with dilemmas. Whereas Philip's own guide is a North American Indian by the name of Wolfsong, mine is elusive, and this may be attributed to the fact that I cannot see his/her face; even after many attempts. It is as though I am strangely denied access to this and, believe me, I have asked!

My guide was present upon summoning him/her, and I asked if he/she would assist me with the experiment.

"I am going to try automatic writing," I said. "Can you please help me in any way possible?"

I wasn't one hundred percent certain as to how the process actually worked, though my guide explained to me, in a knowing sense, that I would have to keep my eyes open and fixed on the page, and to transcribe the channelled results by writing them down in an orderly fashion. He/she then told me that 'trust' was paramount and that I was not to query the pen at all, but to simply record the information without even thinking about it.

It was harder than I thought! To begin with, I was convinced that I was actually influencing the answers myself, frantically scribbling down a few lines and then pausing to reread them; shaking my head and wondering if I was essentially inventing the response; rather than my guide channelling it through.

I was severely reprimanded at this point and reminded to 'trust.' This, I knew, was what I had done during my past life regression - to trust - and so I rethought my approach, adopting the same strategy I had employed during the past life sitting. In effect, I would simply let go and think of myself as being rather like an empty vessel; removing any thoughts from my mind, other than those which would need addressing,.

It worked and, after many hours, days and weeks of asking questions that interested me, I have amassed a healthy dose of answers. I have also recorded them in the order in which they were received for your perusal and I must ask you, if you will, to digest them with an open mind; as fantastic as the results may seem. Try not to be swayed by the rational. Like the universe, the past scholars would rather the conventional theories remain set in stone; denouncing radicals, such as me, to come along and conceitedly revise them.

This experiment was conducted less than ten years ago. I have not, as of yet, resumed the sessions, due to my own literary development which is both time consuming and testing, though I have plans to continue the automatic writing much later in life, and to document the results.

Q. = questions, A. = the response from my guide

Q. Did the Ark of the Covenant really exist?

A. *Indeed. It was an instrument of unimaginable power.*

Q. Was it a gift from God?

A. *No. It was a tool of unprecedented darkness.*

Q. What was its purpose?

A. *Control. The box was used as a weapon to rule the feeble empires of the time.*

Q. Who built it?

A. *Dark forces. What you would deem as being 'Alien.'*

Q. Why did aliens build it? Moses was supposed to have constructed it under the guidance of God.

A. *That is a misconception. The aliens were covert, creating and using the artefact as a means of manipulating the meagre minds of men and to instill fear into the masses, before planning to seize power. Their ship appeared over the alleged Mount Sinai and a great horn was sounded; prompted as a means to attract the holy men's attention and to accept the Ark as a gift; ultimately following its so-called 'Divine Instructions.'*

Q. Wouldn't the holy men have questioned the ship, or creatures delivering the Ark, for that matter?

A. *To them, the ship was a chariot of fire and godly. Also, they would not have questioned such a thing, believing it to be the work of God. The aliens themselves appeared angelic in nature, though this was merely a guise to cover their true selves.*

Q. But the Ark was supposed to have contained the stone tablets - The Ten Commandments - isn't that so?

A. *That was the general belief. But, it was a nemesis of darkness ... a wolf in sheep's clothing.*

Q. You're basically saying that is was a machine of some kind?

A. *Yes. It was artificial, with the aliens managing it from the comfort of their own and secured headquarters.*

Q. What did the aliens actually use it for? I know you say for 'control,' but what exactly was its mission?

A. *To persuade man to believe that it was of holy descent. A division of extra-terrestrials were on the Earth at the time, albeit concealed, though their small numbers alone could not challenge civilisation itself. They were well aware of man's faith in a deity and so, to that effect, masterminded a masquerade as the first stage of a takeover bid. To sway opinion in such a manner, back then, was of vital importance to their plan. They were, in actual fact, impostors; cleverly using the idol (the holy men worshipped) as a means of manipulation. This, in effect, would have elevated them to the status of the Divine, had their plan actually worked.*

Q. For what purpose?

A. *To ultimately enchain civilisation. They were from a galaxy that preferred to use lesser beings to work for them as slaves. Your own history will show that you were no different. In effect, and to put it crudely, they were hoping to utilise cheap labour. These aliens were of a minority, as well as being opportunists; grappling with an idea to control a primitive world and to use it for their own means. Thus, their proposed and deceptive agenda was firmly fixed into place. They believed that, should man be fooled by the holy machine they*

*had constructed, then he would forgo anything and everything
just to serve the ultimate.*

Q. So, we were to become slaves for them, is that it?

A. *Yes. They were already planning to colonise a region of your
world back then, had their strategy not failed.*

Q. These aliens that you talk of sound rather like outlaws to
me. Is that basically what they were? After all, you called
them opportunists.

A. *Yes. Your outlaw approach is rather apt. They were
benevolent to the most gullible at first - those who interacted
with the false God - by extending the hand of friendship. The
allies watched in wonderment and disbelief as their enemies
were effortlessly crushed by the machine, and came to respect
its unimaginable influence.*

Q. What about the burning bush? Were they responsible for
that too?

A. *This, like the Ark, was a tool utilised by the aliens to
influence trust.*

Q. Do you realise how much controversy this may cause? The
Churches will never accept this, renouncing it as utter
twaddle. My own reputation may be put into question.

A. *If you spoke to a burning bush today, would your people
believe you? Or how about a talking donkey? It confounds us
to know that your own kind will accept these fanciful stories,
based on supposed and ancient testimonies, though will
condemn you yourself, should you happen to make contact with
the Divine and subsequently report it.*

But 'they' will not. Know this; the people who embrace the old scriptures do so because they are comfortably out of your timeframe, with absolutely no justifiable proof whatsoever with which to contest.

Q. But there must be some truth to the bible if The Ark of the Covenant was mentioned, surely?

A. *The facts have become muddied and twisted. In any event, the generation of men back then would never have understood such notions as 'beings from other worlds.'*

Q. You mentioned that the aliens failed. Can you elaborate?

A. *Indeed. The cracks began to form when the Ark of the Covenant over-initiated the destruction of people and cities, under the persuasion of the extra-terrestrials. The holy people (the alien's allies and intended slave-race) soon saw it as a monstrosity and began to question its power; contesting that God would never kill his own children so willingly; no matter what beliefs they adopted. It was then condemned as a work of demonic proportion and subsequently apprehended. Disillusioned and out of shame, the holy people buried it in a secured location; hoping against all odds that it's dirty secret would never resurface.*

Q. Couldn't the aliens have used other means to succeed after such a travesty?

A. *The damage was done and they knew enough to realise that no amount of deception could further aid their cause. They had, in any event, underestimated the will of men.*

Q. I wondered how the box could talk to its disciples, as well as kill so easily; this seems plausible ... though fantastic!

A. *The Ark was a conductive element. The power source used to operate it was sophisticated. It did not, as you can quite imagine, contain any tablets.*

A. We *are talking about 'a form' of nuclear energy. This enabled the Ark to swiftly level cities and to burn people who were against its provisional disciples.*

Q. Will we ever find it buried in the Earth, somewhere?

A. *It is possible, though it will be a relic; the technological components installed having, no doubt, disintegrated into nothing more than dust. This will greatly please the present and dedicated disciples; purporting to evade any such notions as extra-terrestrial intervention.*

Q. I would like to move on to the planet Mars. Did it ever contain life?

A. *Planets do not contain life, they support it. But, yes, a civilisation flourished there at one time.*

Q. Were they humanoid?

A. *Do otherworldly creatures have to always resemble man?*

Life forms evolved on the surface of Mars, when the planet was abundant in water, plantation and minerals. They mounted the steps of evolution much earlier than your species.

Q. So, you're saying that they advanced sooner than us.

A. *Indeed. Conversely, upon observing your world during the height of their powers, they did not envy it, as the writers before your time much fancied. The species that resided on the red planet were of a peaceful culture. There is evidence of their*

history still quite visible; with your leading Space Centre
having captured a portion of it on film.

Q. Are you talking about the 'face on Mars?' The monument?

A. *Yes.*

Q. So, it's genuine?

A. *Yes.*

Q. NASA is convinced that it is merely a trick of light.

A. *Ah, but that is what they will only admit. Know this; the leading Space Centre of which I mention is untrustworthy; airbrushing anomalies from photographs that have been taken on the moon and so forth, to make them fit for society and to prevent questions from arising. They will have you believe that there is no life out there, in the great expanse, though they will hypocritically and openly speculate as to the possibility of it; just as long as it doesn't leap out at you.*

Q. I see. Well, that wouldn't surprise me at all. But why keep secrets, especially on this scale?

A. *To amass such data is rewarding for them. They are intent on discovering these things for themselves and they are in coalition with elite investors and military factions; all seeking answers to the question of alternative, intelligent life; along with technological progression via interaction. This establishment is dark, allowing the public to see only what they want them to see.*

Q. So, they are corrupt?

A. *They are a power unto themselves. I would not say that they are corrupt; rather, deceptive.*

Q. Have they discovered life?

A. *Of course. The moon itself represents enormous interest to them, namely because it also supports architectural anomalies which must not, under any circumstances, reach the public.*

Q. Were these also built by the people of Mars?

A. *No. The buildings on the moon are modern bases for another civilisation. Mars perished, many thousands of years ago, in a blast that shattered its stratosphere. Some of the inhabitants escaped in ships, though a good many of them were vapourised by the celestial accident that occurred.*

Q. What accident?

A. *A neighbouring planet was hit by a meteor and disintegrated, great masses of which collided with Mars; with the debris reaching Earth. At this time, Atlantis - the elite continent on your world - was flourishing; though the cataclysm caused huge tidal waves and volcanic eruptions to end this ruling empire, along with the red planet.*

Q. So, there was another planet close by, and which is now missing?

A. *Yes. The great rings of Saturn make up a good part it, with her enormous gravitational pull having attracted its remains into a fixed orbit. Many of your neighbouring worlds were also scarred by the incident; with the Earth, along with Mars, receiving the full brunt of the catastrophe.*

Q. I'd like to move on to ask questions about the Grays, if that's okay with you? These extra-terrestrials are reported to be widespread throughout our present age, though are elusive.

A. *You may ask.*

124

Q. Is there any truth as to their existence?

A. *Indeed.*

Q. Do they represent a threat to us?

A. *No. Had they wished to take over your planet - this being a common fear if such a race were to be malevolent - then they would surly have done so when your civilisation was lesser developed.*

Q. What is their mission here?

A. *To study and collect genetic material from humans in order to assist their own agenda.*

Q. So, they simply kidnap people in the dead of night without our consent, is that it?

A. *If you are referring to the recent reports of abductions, yes.*

On that note, the aliens received consent decades ago. They had, in the past, met with chief diplomats in the USA, in order to present their case; whereby a treaty was forged. For the diplomats, the deal seemed too good to refuse at the time, with them negotiating the exchange of certain technological innovations.

Q. In exchange for what?

A. *Free access to human guinea pigs. The agreement granted the aliens admission to the populace.*

Q. What did the aliens want with people?

A. *I have already told you; study and genetic material.*

Q. By way of experiments, you mean?

A. *Yes. But, their allegiance with the elite humans has now turned sour. Both parties breached their agreements and so the Grays - as you call them - have taken matters into their own hands. They have dismissed the treaty, believing it to be a constraint. The aliens wanted more, in terms of study, with the diplomats becoming equally demanding and so, that is why the treaty is in tatters. Consequently, they continue to study mankind on a regular basis, having discarded further negotiations.*

Q. So, they're outlaws, then?

A. *They are too smart to be outlaws. Through their eyes, they view the governing branch they negotiated with as being both greedy and manipulative. Consequently, the alien faction of whom I speak of has become self-governing.*

Q. What do they want with this genetic material, anyway? Is it to do with cloning?

A. *I am aware that this question has arisen so many times on your world and which requires clarification. Your people are so transfixed with the notion that these advanced creatures (having lost their essence through years of being cloned themselves) wish to create a hybrid - part them/part you - as a means for them to rekindle their genesis. Nevertheless, even if they were able to implement this core agenda, the argument is a conflicting one. Consider this: If you were able to be cloned, then the 'real' you would be the foremost essence, with the double having to gain its own through years of independent experiences. And upon concluding this point, the double would, in effect, be an entirely different person from you; regardless of the physical similarities. To all intents and purposes, it would not be the real you at all; but an estranged and independent doppel-ganger. It would have no record of your love, fears, moods, intelligence and so forth; sharing no mental comparisons with you whatsoever. No amount of genetic tampering can alter this fact.*

Q. I understand. You're basically telling me that, if they were genetically sharing themselves with hybrids in order to breed, then it would not be their true selves; rather, modified impostors?

A. *That is correct. It is so brazenly obvious that I am surprised your scientists have not theorised such disastrous consequences if just such a programme was put into effect on Earth. Do not misread me; the aliens of which you enquire are performing a cloning program of their own, but it is not for this reason. They wish to upgrade ... not to double or treble their numbers.*

Q. Explain.

A. *They will upgrade ... promote ... better themselves to aid their physical development. Their technology may appear staggering, but they are surprisingly weak. They are not infallible. The bodies they harbour must be modified in order for them to become stronger and more versatile. They do not wish to create look-alikes ...rather, improve the suits they currently wear.*

Q. Versatile for what?

A. *To adapt, amongst other things. We believe that they wish to embrace some of your qualities too - qualities which they are stripped of - being that they are of a hive mind. Individuality and independence appeals to them, and they are exploiting these things in greater depth. The modified minds and bodies they plan to perfect may eventually accommodate these values, once they have accomplished their goal.*

Q. You are talking as though they wish to humanise themselves.

A. *No. Let me explain. These aliens were created by a master race. They are not machines; rather, biological automatons that have become smart. They were created to serve their rulers, though many factions deserted them; forsaking service for expansion and understanding. In effect, they developed their own technology and have returned to the world in which their superiors visited centuries ago.*

Q. Earth?

A. *Yes.*

Q. Why our planet?

A. *They are seeking to understand themselves. Because their masters enhanced the natives of your world, they have returned to try and recognize that mutual connection. Since the Grays cannot revisit their fathers, they seek answers here. They are conscious enough to know that the Earth is a vital link to genetic expansion. Their stagnant bodies require modification, as I have already stated, and they feel that this planet of yours is the best chance they have in achieving this goal.*

Q. Okay, so when they've achieved all this - if they do - what then?

A. *They would have perfected stronger bodies and perhaps a clearer understanding of themselves. However, they are eluded by the soul. The advancement of such things, if achieved, will heighten their curiosity and drive them further into seeking additional answers through research.*

Q. Do they have souls?

A. *At present, no. As I said, the aliens were manufactured and this, in turn, has become a problem; due to them exploring answers relating to their origins and ultimate destiny.*

Q. Will they gain souls through these improved bodies of theirs, if they succeed?

A. *Now, this is where it becomes tricky! If the aliens were to perfect such bodies, and to successfully adopt certain values that you take for granted, then an understanding will arise; an understanding that will eventually lead to individualism. This highly complex form of behaviour alone may very well be enough to generate the first spark of a soul and that, in effect, will move them into a radical new age of evolution. You must understand that, at present, they do not encompass love, compassion, hate or fear, for the simple fact that they have no understanding of these sentiments.*

Q. Would they look upon us as being superior, in this regard?

A. *I would not say superior, though they are seeking individualism. Your race, as a whole, intrigues them, and they are looking to adopt certain values that can be useful.*

Q. Wouldn't that make them dangerous to us? If they adopted a newfound sense of independence, wouldn't that also promote ambition, and a means to strive for it?

A. *What ambitious thoughts are you referring to?*

Q. To take over our planet. To wipe us out.

A. *I have already stressed to you that they do not have any plans, at present, to pursue such drastic action. Nonetheless, their own path will be decided by them.*

Q. Yes, but look what freewill has done to us! Not only has is given birth to so many beautiful things, but is has also promoted violence and countless wars which we are still waging today.

A. *The outcome of their future hangs in the balance. We are not qualified to pass judgement on them.*

Q. You say that they are of a hive mind. What exactly does this mean?

A. *I shall explain. A common denominator is that of your bees. the queen bee rules the hive, with her maidens, soldiers and workers following duties that are hardly ever broken. In a sense, the hive becomes one gigantic network, with a single goal in mind; to survive. The bees do not have any independent thoughts of their own, though are instructed by their queen to accomplish this basic principle which is as instinctive as it is vital. The Grays, as you will expect, harbour superior thoughts, though they can be compared with that of the hive.*

Q. Okay, so do they have a queen?

A. *They do not have a queen. They utilise a network - with each and every unit being connected - and all thoughts are derived into one. You may liken this process to that of a basic computer; with it transmitting and sharing data with other terminals. Does this exemplify a feasible account?*

Q. Yes. In any case, their creation is remarkable.

A. *The species that fashioned them, I have already enlightened, were masters of genetic engineering. They were not saints and, on that note, remember this; no race in the history of the cosmos has ever had a virtuous record and yours, I regrettably add, is no exception. The Grays, like yourselves, are survivalists.*

Q. Are the Grays responsible for the cattle mutilations so commonly reported across the world?

A. *Yes. They are analysing human ingestion. The bodies they plan to perfect will require sustenance - being radically different from those they currently wear - and these will demand a biological provision. Due to them gaining material from Earth to pursue this feat, they are testing the cattle for contamination; perhaps attaining a form of nourishment that is similar, though which is free from toxins that humans take for granted, but which may very well prove lethal to them.*

Q. I'd like to move on to questions regarding Heaven.

A. *Yes.*

Q. What is it like?

A. *In effect, it is what you want it to be.*

Q. Are you saying that it is based on our personal vision of an ideal world?

A. *To a degree, yes. Heaven is not a planet, but a dimension.*

Q. Can you define exactly what a dimension is?

A. *I shall try and clarify this point as best I can. A dimension is a pocket of time and space that is invisible to the naked eye. Heaven is rather like this and it encompasses your world. Basically, you could say that we are virtually next door to you. Rather like a radio or television signal, it cannot be seen or touched - being undetectable - but it is there all the same. It dwells on a frequency that your scientific instruments cannot detect.*

Q. How can a frequency be a living mass of something like Heaven?

A. *You are defining this wavelength in terms of being artificial; though the example I have given cannot be understood wholly by yourself for the simple fact that you cannot appreciate my interpretation. Thought is energy, and this energy resides in the dimension in which we occupy; though it is not synthetic. Your researchers have already tried to contact us using radio equipment; modulating the frequency of their electromagnetic emissions in an attempt to discover our realm, though their instruments are far too weak to accomplish this, as of yet.*

Q. I have read books, whereby people believe they have actually captured photographs of Heaven, using state-of-the-art radio equipment. I've seen them.

A. *And what did you make of these photographs?*

Q. To be honest, they looked false.

A. *Then why are you addressing the issue?*

Q. To ask your own personal opinion of such claims.

A. *Let me assure you of one thing. No human on your world has ever captured a photographic image of Heaven. This very notion is deceptive. Also, if they were able to capture pictures of us, then surely they'd be able to speak with us too, as freely as you would speak with friends or relatives on a telephone.*

Q. But Mediums have been able to contact you?

A. *Yes, they have, and quite successfully. The genuine types are hard workers, having expanded their consciousness to attune themselves to our wavelength. But, with all their might, they bring scraps through; though it is enough evidence to corroborate our very existence. Gifted or trained minds are far more effective than mere machinery, as far as this argument is concerned.*

Q. So, you could arguably say that if it wasn't for Mediums, we'd never know of your dimension.

A. *Firstly, the Earth is rather like a learning centre, with you and billions of others having incarnated from our realm to experience new emotions, skills and goals. And, upon each incarnation, it would not be beneficial for you to recall your origins; that of our dimension. Nonetheless, it is accessible to a degree - as your people have clearly demonstrated through clairvoyance - though the power of this is subtle. You, as a species, are not really meant to touch Heaven; only having complete access to it upon graduation and departure.*

Q. So, we choose to incarnate on Earth?

A. *That is so.*

Q. What about stillborns, babies that die, children who perish, along with a whole host of other disheartening and terrible things that happen to so many of our juveniles?

A. *Now, I would like to make a very clear point here and, however harsh it may seem to you, you must accept it with an understanding that you, as a race, are immortal; albeit not on a physical level. We have no control over your world and no way of preventing stillborns, diseases, accidents, disasters and other horrors that plague it. Since you are in the physical flesh, you are at the mercy of the unlimited variables that may occur during your lifetime on the planet and we have heard it, more often than not, that people question why disasters strike, wars begin, deaths occur and so on. We cannot manage or intervene with your affairs simply because you are left to your own devices; your planet being exclusively entrusted to you. As unsympathetic as this may seem, you must embrace it with strength and dignity.*

Q. So, you're basically saying that we are at the mercy of our own fate, while on Earth.

A. *Indeed. Death is a terrible thing due to emotions and loss - and we fully understand this - though we cannot be blamed for it. It is one of the many prices to pay, in order to experience love and hate, pleasure and pain, inspiration, good fortune, etc. For example, some souls here - who have never incarnated on your world - do not understand what it is like to feel hot and cold, or what an orange must taste like. Because they have never subjected themselves to such sensations, they know no different. But for you, it is commonplace.*

Q. Are these things important?

A. *They are to you, because you choose to return.*

Q. Return to what? Most of the time, I fret over how unfair people are treated in the world. There is so much poverty, hunger and hatred. War is never far off, either!

A. *Your planet is beautiful, though your race has an insatiable desire to pillage what it can for profit. Pollution is an old tune now - and an exhausting one - though your own governments are blinkered to the fact that, in time, things will change - and for the worst - if action is not implemented. They hypocritically announce their concerns during periods of advancing towards a representative-state; though fail to act when they are in power. Their words are only instigated as a ruse to gain advancement and material wealth, with little regard for others. Nevertheless, nearer the time and when the atmospheric conditions of your world deteriorate even further, your ruling factions will then have no choice but to initiate dire measures for survival. By this time, it may be too late.*

134

Q. You can't argue with politicians and, even if you address with them the issue of global warming - or whatever dire problems we face - they'll skirt around the question and palm it off for another day, which never comes!

A. *We are straying from your questions regarding Heaven!*

Q. I have to ask this, though I have already reached a conclusion of my own: Is there such a thing as a 'Devil?'

A. *No.*

Q. What about 'Hell?'

A. *Your definition of 'Hell' is that of stagnation, misery and sin. In effect, this is so, though I can assure you that there is no devilish demon to complement the scenes of which you imagine Hell to be. There is a place that is as foul as it is frightening, and it is here where the emotionally corrupt preside. This place I speak of is abysmal, with the souls having to come to terms with their depraved actions while on the Earth; though I must stress that there is always hope for them; albeit on an extremely restrained level.*

Q. What does it look like?

A. *I shall not answer that question.*

Q. Okay, so; what about people like Adolf Hitler? Is he to be granted amnesty?

A. *Some souls are destroyed.*

Q. You're saying that Adolf Hitler has been destroyed!

A. *I am not quoting this to satisfy the generations which he persecuted and exterminated, though it is better that we leave your question best alone. All I am prepared to say is that he has been abolished.*

Q. I'm very glad to hear it.

A. *It is not pleasant to wish this type of conclusion on any of God's children, though this individual was twisted beyond all measure. His doom was sealed upon the destruction of innocent people and the bitterness of which he harboured against all that was not part of his preferred regimental dictatorship. On this note, there are a number of political leaders on your world at present who will also share the same fate, when they physically expire.*

Q. Can you name them?

A. *That would not be fair on their part and would place you in a very awkward position. On the other hand, two of these warmongers will surprise you to the point of disbelief!*

Q. Not even a hint?

A. *No. However, and as I have stated, the two primed for abolishment have cleverly heralded the masses into believing their own war efforts to be just when, in actual fact, they have secretly used their political clout for their own ethnic cleansing programme; together with personal economic growth. It is a sad state of affairs, but there you have it.*

Q. I'd like to ask if you, or your people, have actually seen God.

A. *Your reference to God is based on a life form with a physical description. In answer to your question, no, we have not seen God and let me explain why. God is matter and anti-matter. God is the physical and the mental. God is the positive and the negative. So, as you can quite understand, 'The Divine'*

*does not have a face - as you would prefer - for us to depict.
Rather, it encompasses the all.*

Q. He's energy then?

A. *God is everything. 'The Divine' is neither man nor woman
either, being that it has never incarnated on your world, or any
other for that matter. In essence, it is genderless; bearing no
physical relation to any one given thing at any one given time.*

Q. But I thought we were supposed to have been formed in the
image of God.

A. *That is a completely biased assumption based on your
ancient testimonies. On reflection, you have humanised God to
the point of believing that you are the only species to have been
formed by 'The Divine's' hand when, in actual fact, you are
alienating the very notion of this force having created other
beings besides yourselves. Your Earth is, for the best part, a
homo-sapiens segregation guild.*

Q. So, you're basically saying that God is everything, right
down to the last atom?

A. *Yes.*

Q. Did God create the universe?

A. *We believe so. And, before you contest me on the point of us
supposedly being the fountain of knowledge, let me correct you.
Even we, with all our insights and wisdom, cannot see or know
everything, and this is another fallacy in which you humans
have adopted. We learn here, just as you learn there; it is as
simple as that. Prevalent questions, such as the creation of the
physical universe, as well as our residing dimensions, are still
to be explored. It would be a dull thing, wouldn't you agree, if
we had all the answers to all these riddles.*

A. *Regarding that point; it forces us to seek the answers through advancement; stimulating our minds to fathom the unfathomable, to contest the incontestable and to achieve the unachievable. Progression is paramount and, without it, we would become stagnant.*

This was as much as I was able to glean from my Guide. On reflection, it still leaves many questions to be explored and, not having continued with the automatic writing for some years now, I have a wealth of queries to put forward. Such as; how exactly did God create the Universe and was the Spirit world in existence long before it. Also, how old is Heaven and where did it come from? And, if the answer is based on God's divine participation ... then who created God? It is a paradox and one, I suspect, that we are not meant to know. Like the chicken and the egg, what came first? My Guide informed me that we must search for these answers ourselves through a step-by-step process, whereby evolution may eventually access certain keys to certain locks that contain hints, or solutions.

I suppose it is rather like us handing a transistor radio to a caveman, with him being unable to comprehend it. In hindsight, it would appear that we are currently in a similar dilemma, with us having to advance even more in order to grasp and appreciate the fascinating questions I have addressed.

The process of automatic writing was hard and mentally challenging for me to accomplish and, even now, I look back and wonder as to how accurate the results were. In effect, I have no evidence to support the claims made by those in the Spirit world, though I am positive that the information was handed to me in a coherent and truthful manner.

Make of it what you will. I have plans, nonetheless, to produce a book based on the conversations I have shared with my Guide; though will endeavour to obtain a lot more answers to the questions that puzzle me, and other like minds.

Chapter Fourteen

A Prayer is Answered

When you are at your lowest ebb, there is always hope; no matter how distant it may seem. Because Philip and I were hard at work on our mechanical dog creation 'Magnus the Micro-Mutt' during the 90's, we had developed a fair amount of concept drawings, paintings, together with stories based on his adventures. But, the dog was being rejected left, right and centre. For years, we tried everything imaginable, approaching literary agents, publishers, film companies and even computer software corporations, to no avail.

It was in the summer of 2004 when Spirit actually answered a prayer for me. During a weekend in Norfolk and staying at my cousin's house, along with my Mother, I had a chat with Spirit; though it was a heated argument on my part! With my cousin and Mum having decided to go shopping on the Saturday, I opted to stay home - not feeling too good due to a headache - and, upon them leaving, I sat myself down in the lounge and thought about Magnus.

I was angry! The decade had been fraught with disappointments; with us striving to make Magnus fit in the 20th Century due to him seemingly being too radical for the time. The character was joined by a handsome Captain - hopefully appealing to the girls - along with a young Princess (being the owner of the dog) and who also had a secret girly-crush on the dashing bodyguard. Out of interest, the bodyguard was modelled after our best friend, Matthew J. Bailey, who we have known for over twenty years and who kindly agreed for the character to be physically fashioned in his image. But, nobody would undertake the project. Philip and I had, by this time, amassed hundreds of rejection letters.

During this disheartening decade, *The Times & Citizen* newspaper in Bedford had written a beautiful spread about the dog, which featured detailed illustrations of him and his friends. This, in turn, prompted a company to approach us, with the intention of turning him into a computer game. We were hopeful and the corporation supplied us with a detailed dossier of what they planned for the Micro-Mutt. However, the deal turned sour and the company sent us, of all things, a rejection letter; informing us that, due to the dog not being as popular as Sooty or Noddy, they could not pursue the project. I telephoned them and spoke with the Director, kindly reminding him that they had approached us in the first instance. He was patient and, after offering his apologies, proposed to purchase the rights to Magnus for £200. I was insulted, though kindly turned him down.

Later, and as I mentioned, the dog was handled by a manager who, as it turned out, wanted complete ownership of the copyright. It was an utter sham; being the straw that broke the camel's back. Philip and I reluctantly decided to put Magnus on the backburner, having temporarily exhausted all avenues and ideas. I should think that ten years was enough to verify our need to consider new options, as well as to rethink a new tactic; if only to get Magnus out into the world.

I sat there, in the lounge of my cousin's house, and spoke to 'them upstairs'. It was a curt conversation, and I actually accused them of letting us down. I told them that we had given the Magnus project one hundred percent - having sacrificed most of our spare time on it - only to have it thrown back in our faces. And, not just once, but hundreds of times! Philip and I had self published him - having invested a few thousand pounds over the course of the decade, though we

THE ROCK BOTTOM TWINS

Boogle & Buff Kings-Million revel in their dodgy get-rich-quick scheme as their domestic robot, RAMSHACK, begins his cleaning chores in the old hag's Manor House.

Published by Pegasus Books - © 2006 Ronald & Philip Kinsella

had failed. It felt personal; having achieved so little, along with being rejected by every publisher conceivable.

And then something peculiar happened. As I ranted and raved at the misery of our literary downfall, I actually felt a presence in the room. Somebody, I was utterly convinced, was standing behind my chair; for I had to do a double take ... only to find nothing occupying the spot in question. But somebody was listening with the patience of a saint and the kindness of an Angel and, although I could not see this invisible entity, I knew with certainty that it was there all the same; absorbing my failures and despairs like a sponge.

I was being listened to!

I have to say that, after my emotional outburst, I actually felt better. I wiped my tears away and left it at that. But something was seeding within my mind and, although I did not acknowledge it at the time, I am now convinced that it was Spirit's way of assisting me; by way of boosting a new plan of action. And, my goodness, the key to the problem came within twenty four hours and which hurled me into a newfound sense of enthusiasm and determination. For me, it was the answer to a prayer.

With Mum driving me back home that Sunday, the weather was beautiful. It was during this time in the car that I was envisioning a bold new project, as well as the exciting possibilities it offered. By the time we stopped off at a pub midway, I had concocted a fictional story in my head which was as simple as it was amusing.

Magnus was to be suspended for the time being, to make way for 'The Rock Bottom Twins.' This in no way undermined the dog, as both Philip and I have a great fondness for him, though the new project promised to act as a stepping stone; hopefully guaranteeing him his golden day in the future.

Thanks to Spirit, we managed to pull this new project off, though it was not without its hiccups and backlashes; taking almost two years to finally gain interest.

At the pub and sipping my beer, I saw Boogle and Buff Kings-Million; fat, argumentative, sixty year-old identical twin brothers, living in a rambling old house and having virtually squandered all their savings on booze, rich teacakes along with a whole host of other guzzling luxuries. In my mind, I observed their Bank Manager (Mr Quids) telephoning the grumpy old so-and-so's, informing them that, due to their lavish lifestyles, they were officially broke. I envisioned the pair concocting a dastardly plan of action in order to rectify their atrocious state of affairs. Being too lazy to work, they rekindle their old magic for electronic engineering and assemble a mechanical man, with the intention of him acting as a skivvy, to earn them a crust-or-two; with an old biddy's Manor House - down the road - being his first port of call. By the time I had finished my drink, I saw the robot, RAMSHACK, trashing the Manor House - due to his dodgy programming - with the twins ultimately paying the price for their idleness; their ludicrous get-rich-quick-scheme subsequently backfiring.

Spirit advised me to look deep within myself and to poke fun at my own sad state of affairs, including Philip's, and to encompass us in a twisted tale of desperation and laughter. Thus, the twin characters were born and, upon returning home, I spent three solid days punching out a 64 paged story for children; subsequently adding concept pictures of the grumpy duo, their mechanical servant along with the old biddy Mrs Tightbelly occupying the Manor House. Due to Philip being away on holiday, I waited for him to return, before reading him the script and, upon doing so, he laughed so much that the tears were actually streaming down his face. I knew then that we had something tangible. We then set about lengthening and revising the story, adding detailed illustrations in a portfolio-style package, before beginning the arduous task of searching for a publisher.

By this time, Philip was a professional working Medium and was, more-than-not, doing 'The Rounds' as we fondly coined the phrase; demonstrating his clairvoyance at local and general Spiritualist Churches throughout the region, and developing a sound reputation for himself. I remembered asking him if, at some point in the future, 'The Rock Bottom Twins' would be accepted by a publisher. He merely nodded, though would say no more on the matter.

We began to send the book out to publishers, though they were being returned just as fast. Unperturbed, we dispatched more, finally gaining the interest of a Literary Agent in Edinburgh. Delighted, we tweaked the story, adding a few more detailed illustrations to accompany the book, before sending it to our potential representatives. Nine months later, they rejected it, informing us that the story was too 'wacky and off-the-wall' for their taste and consequently would not be making an offer. Naturally, we were gutted, though continued to send the work out, nonetheless.

"You've sent me stuff before. In fact, you've made a number of submissions ... please do not send me any more work."

These were the exact words of one Literary Agent in London and, having read the email, Philip and I were flabbergasted. To my mind, 'The Rock Bottom Twins' deserved a little more credit, considering the obnoxious email we received from the equally obnoxious man. I immediately sent an apology to him, kindly informing him that we would never send another piece of work to his office. To this day, we have kept our word.

It became apparent to me, back then, that the children's book market centred, more-than-not, on mushy teenage heroics with predictable endings. I was even incensed at some of the twaddle I happened to pick up during my visits to the local bookshops; observing the illustrations in these books appearing to have been composed by elephant's armed with paintbrushes in their trunks! And, before I am rapped on the knuckles for being too brash or vengeful, I must first state that this conclusion was based on rational observation at how the publishing monopoly worked. They were not, for the best part, willing to set their sights outside the current trends; if only to chance something quite diverse.

To prove a point, one major author at the time (the queen of children's literature as Philip and I fondly regard her) astounded the world by taking a different approach to something rather challenging; with her agent and publisher deciding to take a chance. And yet, when her beautiful books were published, copycats rallied around to take a bite out of her phenomenal success, with their own renderings flanking the bookshelves. This, we knew, was a typical approach and one which was infuriating. Thankfully, the queen of literature remains distinguished; with her crown firmly fixed on her head.

We were in for a very rough ride! We started to post our book to America, and this became costly, having to also include International Reply Coupons as payment for stamps should the work prove unworthy; which it did. New York did not want it, and neither did some of the other leading states. Consequently, we had to return to the British publishers and agents; remembering to avoid the obnoxious one in London!

Some were kind and some were sympathetic, though 'The Rock Bottom Twins' was beginning to invoke a certain irony about it. As the rejections mounted, I began to fret; fearing the worst. It was at this point when I actually doubted my own literary style - even the illustrations - and that I should perhaps give the entire thing up. It was a soul destroying thought, and I hated myself for it as much as I hated the people who could not see the vision of our fictional world. To make matters even worse, people at work were beginning to jibe us over our failures; knowing full well of our past literary attempts.

"Made your millions, yet? Got a bestseller in the works, have you?"

We had to endure this taunting madness for some time, remaining steadfast in our efforts to find someone, somewhere, who would undertake the project. Philip had just finished writing a book about his own spiritual development entitled 'Reaching for the Divine' - submitting it to Capall Bann - with 'The Rock Bottom Twins' having topped 60 rejection letters. Nonetheless, and during the summer of 2005, Spirit once again intervened to give me a sign of hope.

Both Philip and I were sitting in the garden during a pleasant evening, both sharing a bottle of red wine. It was during this time of relaxation when he turned to face me, ready to impart some interesting news.

"My Guide, Wolfsong, is telling me that 'The Rock Bottom Twins' will be accepted by a publisher, before Christmas of this year," he informed. "I'm seeing a middle-aged man with a caring face and it will be the illustrations themselves that will clinch the deal; somehow rekindling his own childhood. The company will be based in England."

He said it so casually and confidently that I was a little thrown for words! I reminded him that it was already August and that both publishers and agents alike took months to respond, due to the mass of submissions they received on a weekly basis. Also, most of them were women; a sound fact considering the countless enquiries I had made by phone, emails and letters. I just couldn't get my head around the fact that we would receive a contract before Christmas, though I thanked him nonetheless and left it at that.

Two months later, a gentleman from Pegasus requested the rest of the book and, prior to Christmas, *'Reaching for the Divine'* was accepted by Capall Bann. Shortly after that, an offer was made to publish *'The Rock Bottom Twins'* and it was a surreal and joyous moment. We celebrated it with a bottle of Champaign which Mum had purchased just for the occasion.

When the books were released a year later, we had signing sessions organized at WHSmith, Waterstones and other stores, though trouble was already brewing at one particular bookshop. As it happened, this store was dominated by two pushy women who did not, so it seemed, like the idea of local authors having achieved moderate success. They had already sent a good number of people away upon requesting *'The Rock Bottom Twins;'* merely informing them that they did not stock it and that it was not available.

This, in itself, was intolerable and, having received numerous complaints from customers, Philip decided to take action.

He went to visit the shop, taking a poster along with him with the intention of them advertising the book in their window. But, upon meeting the two women in question, they were having none of it. In fact, they told him that they would have to consult with Head Office first, before presenting the placard; informing him that red tape had to be cut. The best they could do, they said, was to hang it in their private staffroom, though Philip blatantly declined this heartless offer. He then asked why they were sending people away.

"We don't stock it," they replied. "We can't order it and it's not available."

Philip then explained to them that other bookshops didn't appear to have trouble with orders and sales, though they refused to comment any further. He then requested one of

148

their Sales Assistants, who was stationed at the till point, to check their computer for availability. The man did so, though under protest from one of the assertive women, only to find that the book was indeed orderable. The Sales Assistant swung the screen around and kindly acknowledged this fact to Philip who, by this time, was seething.

"Right, I want your names!" he demanded, turning to face the woman. "Your bookshop can obtain it and I am going to find out why it is that you're sabotaging sales."

We contacted our publisher, explaining the problem to them, and they approached the company's Head Office, informing them of the unacceptable behaviour the book was receiving from the said outlet. Something must have transpired, because the bookshop eventually received them; though we found out later that the two women - who were passing themselves off as Managers - were stuffing them under the till point, refusing to place them on the bookshelves. When we actually spoke with the genuine Manager, it became clear to us that he was evidently too weak to contest the clout in which his formidable employees administered.

I was infuriated at the fact of our book being hidden away, though was powerless to stop these blinkered employees. And, to prove it was personal, another author from Pegasus enjoyed a signing session there, with her posters proudly gracing the windows and her books promptly lining the shelves. We were very pleased for her, but fuming at our own treatment.

The only thing that temporarily stopped this outrageous conduct was when Philip and I appeared on 'About Anglia' T.V., who kindly did a feature about us and our books, and broadcast it in 2007. The article was extremely constructive, with the interviewer informing the public of our past failures, along with sharing live footage of us working on our illustrations. Subsequently, this led to a few interviews on some of the local radio stations who were, we have to say, wonderful in promoting our work. On that note, Philip and I have been extremely lucky with the Bedfordshire Newspapers; these publishers having always made certain of us gaining a measure of endorsement and of which we are tremendously grateful.

But, the disobliging bookshop in question was to use a trump card in order to make us look like idiots, and regrettably their little trick worked quite beautifully. It was personal, once again, and beggars belief as to why. We had not, to our minds, ever crossed anyone's path and, indeed, did not know of anyone bearing a grudge; though it might be wise to reflect that even Jesus - with all his kindness and courage - faced enemies!

In 2007, Philip and I had completed the second book in the 'The Rock Bottom Twins' series and were incredibly honoured to have had it endorsed by the world's leading Science Fiction/Fantasy artists, Boris Vallejo and Julie Bell. Their artwork is simply staggering! In fact, both of these wonderful souls have been extremely encouraging to us, boosting our own confidence and determination. They are also the authors of many books and have done work for cooperates such as Nike and Coco Cola, to name but a few of their remarkable achievements.

In this second edition, Boogle and Buff hear of a diamond belonging to an African tribe occupying a part of the Congo, and the diamond is sizable! Believing it to have been entrusted to them by a shimmering elephant god (for the freak diamond resembles one of these bulls) the tribe await his return; their own history dictating that he will appear from the stars to reclaim his glittering jewel.

Boogle and Buff hit on a devious plan in order to get their grubby little hands on the irresistible gem. Borrowing money from a wealthy investor, they construct a colossal mechanical elephant with the intention of travelling on him through the perilous jungle; willing and eager to palm him off as the tribe's mythical deity, in order to obtain the diamond. It is a tale of adventure, robots and danger, and our publisher was extremely enthusiastic.

Upon its launch in 2008, WHSmith and Waterstones were marvellous, promoting it with the pride and dignity of any first and exciting fable. Wrapped up in the enthrallment of the new book, Philip and I decided to let bygones be bygones, and so approached the dubious bookshop - which had snubbed the first - eagerly setting a date for a signing session. It was agreed.

With the other stores having received their editions in time for the signings, you would have thought, wouldn't you, that our nemesis would have heartily concurred.

With the planned Saturday almost upon us, we received a call from the Manager of the bookshop in question.

"Your books haven't turned up yet," he informed. "I'll ring you again, later in the week, to let you known the situation."

I emailed our publisher, if only to find out if they had received just such an order from the bookshop. After a while, they confirmed to us that no such requisition had been made. On the Saturday of our signing session, I telephoned the shop at 9.00am sharp, in the hope of the books having been express-delivered for the event.

"They're still not here," the Manager merely apologized. "I'm afraid you'll have to call off the signing session, and reconvene it when we receive the books."

Philip and I had to telephone everyone we could think of who had kindly offered to attend the session. Not only was it embarrassing, it was also another nail in the coffin as far as the store was concerned. We knew, with absolute certainty, that it was sabotage on their part ... and not just the second time, either! Shortly after that, Philip was to promote his own book 'Reaching for the Divine' - and they trumped up the same old story, informing him that they could not obtain them in time for the signing. As it happened, he was able to gain them just before the event; no thanks to the shop.

I am pleased to inform you that a new woman is present at the bookshop and who is extremely polite and helpful. You'll also be happy to know that our books currently grace the shelves, thanks to her.

The pettiness of it astounds me. We, as human beings, have to fight to gain any measure of reputation or success, toiling away at dreams; only to be challenged by jealousy and a desire, by others, for you to fail. People can be cruel. And, when you're ultimately climbing the commercial ladder one painful step at a time, there is always someone willing to shake you off it.

I shall never forget the spiteful comment made by one particular employee at the large department store where both Philip and I work; a man who could be hot and cold and who had annoyingly coined the phrase; "Made your millions yet?" A radio journalist had arrived within the building to inter-view us over 'The Rock Bottom Twins.' We couldn't do it at home due to a time restriction on his behalf, so he kindly agreed to prerecord the session at our place of work and within the training room upstairs. Having to sign in on the ground floor, I accompanied him, while Philip shot upstairs to organize the room. Our rival, of whom I mentioned, was seated within the security office with his mate, just before the signature booth. He asked the journalist something to the effect of:

"Come to interview the twins, then?"

"Yes," the journalist smiled.

"It won't take you long ... it's only a small book, isn't it, Ronald?"

Having signed in, the journalist then followed me upstairs. He turned to face me and sincerely asked:

"Do you often get that?"

"Yes," I nodded. "Quite often."

Life certainly has its trials and when you are faced with such adversity, it unfortunately hardens the heart. Whether it's a good thing or bad thing, I'm not sure. However, what I am certain of is the fact that, when you strive to achieve something, you must first embrace hardship. Nothing comes easy, no matter what, and it may be a learning curve in itself - depending on the circumstances - to make you a far better and stronger person. Nonetheless, mental pain is just as damaging as physical, if not far worse.

*   *   *

Before I conclude the book, I shall first try and explain to you why it is that I believe both Philip and I adopted these creative elements long before we were born on Earth. I am utterly convinced that, as souls, we have pursued a continual fascination for artistic elements that may well be reflections of the world in which we originated; that of the Spiritual dimension. On reflection, I have surmised that these beautiful activities we engage are mere whispers of a greater realm, a realm that is as magnificent as our own cosmos in which we, at present, hardly understand. It is of little wonder why conventional scientists refuse to speculate as to the existence of such a godly kingdom, considering they are ultimately eluded by the creation of the physical one.

Chapter Fifteen

Twin Souls

As children, Philip and I never did watch much television. In any event, there were only a few channels available at the time, though we did enjoy Rupert Bear - the characters all being puppets - which was aired on ITV and which had a catchy theme tune to it, the likes of which we still remember to this very day. Even in 1973, Rupert instilled a fascination for us, not least because he, along with his friends, was unreal. We did not imagine Rupert Bear coming alive after the shows, to join us in the garden - which would have been smashing - whereby we could go on adventures with him because, as I have stated, Philip and I lacked the emphasis to conjure such creative desires; being too young to do so. Nevertheless, the bear was a charming wonderment and an ingenious creation for children.

We didn't have imaginary friends either, and I can quite understand why. Having been born together, the people watching over us in Spirit knew enough to realise that our own company was sufficient to offer companionship and motivation. Nevertheless, it is hugely evident to point out that many children, especially those who are single, unremittingly embrace such entities; talking, playing and interacting with them on a daily basis; believing them to be as real as you and I. This, I understand, is the Spirit world's way of intervening with them when stimulation is required, and they can come in many guises; no doubt able to imitate even the lovable Rupert Bear, should the occasion arise, depending on the child's subconscious preference.

I heard an account from Philip a few years back, after conducting private readings for a group of people one evening, which offered food for thought. One lady informed him that her daughter would often talk to an invisible friend, in her bedroom, and she'd, more-than-not, hear her laughing and squealing with delight. It got to the stage where the mother would leave her own bedroom door open at night - with the landing light left on - if only to keep a vigilant eye open, should her little one applaud the arrival of her undetectable chum. She told Philip that this action was based purely on curiosity, not wishing to break her daughter's puzzling euphoria.

One particular night, the mother was sleeping with her daughter in the main bedroom - the child having been unsettled for one reason or another - only to find herself unexpectedly rousing. Upon opening her eyes, she suddenly noticed something hiding behind her door. Shocked, she sat bolt upright in bed and, to her absolute disbelief, watched as an old and tiny, bald-headed man - having tufts of hair flurried up at the sides - poke his head around the corner to greet her.

She told Philip that the man's face was compassionate.

"He just said, 'Oh!' in a comical sort of way, as though expressing his own surprise at seeing me, and waggled out to reveal himself, hands defensively propped up in silent exclamation. His entire demeanour was highly amusing and innocent. It was at this point when I noticed him being smartly dressed, wearing a Granddad-style shirt, complete with well-groomed trousers supported by braces, along with a pair of neat shoes. The fashion was predated."

The old man then turned around, theatrically jiggling through the hallway, before disappearing.

It is evident in itself to assume that the elderly trespasser wanted the mother to see him; if only to belay her growing concerns for her daughter's peculiar behaviour when left alone. Contemplating this, he took an awful chance and it is of little wonder that the mother wasn't hysterical, though she did report to Philip that she was shocked, all the same. It is, I feel, a charming, though disconcerting portrayal of the power of Spirit and how it is they are able to physically manifest themselves into our realm, when wisdom permits.

Inherent memories of the Spirit world are, I feel, still strong in children; of which slowly dissipate as the juvenile becomes accustomed with the new and physical realm.

Creativity began when Philip and I were around eight years old, and this was prompted by our Auntie Denise who used to bring us reams upon reams of plain paper to draw on. The excitement we felt at the time, armed with pencils, to create visual stories - yes stories - was unprecedented and we loved the visits of this generous lady who reinvigorated our imaginations. I say reinvigorated because, as it happens, we were drawing talking aircrafts landing on islands and conversing with, of all things, sharks! And, upon recently defining the images, I have come to conclude that we were effectively portraying metaphors of Heaven; the delicate residue of it being evocative in our young, human minds.

The aircraft depicts flight - or us having descended from a higher realm - while the island represents the Earth. As for the sharks - well, they embody a known and feared creature of the planet - symbolising the harsh trials to come, while gracing the physical realm. As children, we were too young to comprehend such images, though they were drawn on compulsion, with no understanding of their significance.

This artistic compulsion led to more astonishing creations. Philip and I would turn our toy box upside-down in our bedroom and place it in the centre of the room to act as a body. We then set about making a head, using our Lego box, which we propped up at one end of it; finally balancing our toy lorries at the rear of the smaller one to act as ears. This, in effect, produced a make-believe robot dog and, would you believe me if I told you that both Philip and I actually spoke to it!

This only ignited a fevered urge, on our part, to derive the impossible; robots being our weakness. We had this insatiable desire to imagine, draw and write about them all the time; our unshakable hunger for alternative, fantastical friends never, to this day, having left us. Whether they reside in Heaven is not known, though I suspect that the people there can have almost anything they wish - within reason - and that the world in which Philip and I came from must surely embrace these fanciful metal associates. In any event, they are not new; having been envisioned ever since the industrial revolution took effect, and so represent a longing for humans to strive for an alternative workforce.

When we moved to Hazlebury Crescent in Luton, Granddad Kinsella kindly gave Philip and I his record player - a large, though tidy cabinet with the deck accessed beneath a nifty lid - and was, I have to say, absolutely beautiful. It was also equipped with a radio, though the vinyls were a major source of entertainment. Philip and I would shut ourselves away in our room and play records for the best part of the weekend. Not only that, we would pretend we were actors, giving each other performances to the tunes of Star Wars, Tomita, various 80's hits, to name but a few. One record that delighted us beyond all measure was a vinyl that Granddad had given us, along with the player. *The Ventures - Best of pop Sounds -* must have been replayed hundreds, if not thousands of times, and there was a track on it that encapsulated the very essence of escapism; ironically labelled 'Escape.'

During our time at the dreaded High School, there was an extremely kind and distinct-looking Maths teacher by the name of Miss Horton. Miss Horton was also humourous; having an unforgettable voice. Her very persona intrigued us both beyond all measure and, in our twisted worlds of fantasy, we'd go home and play 'Escape' - armed with a large and stylish ray-gun belonging to Philip - with Miss Horton being the major character in a scene aboard a star ship. It was a comical portrayal of the teacher in pursuit of two charming, if not difficult pupils; wishing to apprehend them for their unruly behaviour. Philip would suspend the stylus over the track before I presented my piece, with me hiding behind our wardrobe door - lifting a leg up into the air as high as I could in readiness for Miss Horton's quest - before he carefully lowered the needle onto the designated track. It was just Miss Horton, with her natty ray-gun, hunting the duo down in an effort to stop them from reaching an escape pod; to ultimately make a quick departure.

Madness? No, I believe this was what we were initially meant to do due to our Spiritual paths, though the pupils at school would have laughed their heads off should they have found out what the weird Kinsella twins got up to in their spare time. In any event, we dismissed the real world as a perplexing hindrance; unwilling to embrace it for fear of rejection. The warped worlds we conjured were far more interesting than humanity's empire, and we felt secure in our wishful bubbles. Even back then, I knew - along with Philip - that we were, and in some strange way, destined to create things. How and why are questions within themselves, though the realm in which we departed, to arrive here, must surely be fantastic; the residue of which unreservedly seeped through us, unable to be capped.

Flying became the next obsession. We would both look out of our window and imagine ourselves having developed a machine that could whip us through the air with minimal fuss. We possessed a squat and lengthy table and so, propping two chairs on it within the room - one behind the other - we'd sit on our makeshift craft and pretend to take flight; passing through the clouds and reaching the sky's zenith. We'd set our toy soldiers and tanks out on the carpet, imagining them to be diminutive figures, as we soared above them, pulling invisible levers and twisting imperceptible dials to adjust speed and altitude. For us, it seemed real, and only inflamed our imaginary juices.

Our sister, Chris, had a room at the back of the house. She also had a fantastic collection of dolls, teddy-bears and other lifeless friends which we would play with. At night, we'd sometimes go into Chris's room (where she had a sizeable plastic play-house set in a corner) and, armed with torches, we'd switch off the main light and enter this portable dwelling; placing the dolls and teddy bears in snug positions and feeling homely and secure inside the enclosure. There was something fascinating about playing inside a house within a house and the surreal joy it offered was beyond measure. I used to look out of the plastic window, at the darkness outside, and imagine monsters creeping around; waiting to nab us. However, they could not penetrate our safe abode and, besides, we could hide behind the large smiling teddy bears should the fiends decide to enter. We'd have pretend tea parties with our inanimate friends and then dare each other to go out in the dark; sometimes throwing an unfortunate doll out of the door to see if the wretched beasts would gobble her up; these toys always suffering the worst!

At the time, the very notion of immortality on a soul level, along with incarnation, would have seemed foreign and laughable to us, and yet we naively embraced our alternative worlds to distance ourselves from the alien one which encompassed us; for it truly was alien! To add credence to this observation, I must point out that, as juveniles, we were never really comfortable with people - being extremely shy -

and that the customs and routines of humanity bewildered us. It has taken many years for the introvert part of us to expire; having gained confidence and reassurance as we learn more about our world and the people within it.

My uncle is convinced that, being twins, we are two halves of the whole; that is to say, we have been split from the original source - the soul - to learn and adapt quicker. This I have to disagree with - although it is a fascinating concept - if only to point out that Penny mentioned both Philip and I having lived on Atlantis during its golden era. And we were not twins then. If he is correct, then what of triplets? Personally, I am inclined to believe that the natural birth of twins may represent the end of a long journey for them on a soul level; having incarnated together for eons, with the final physical mirror image signifying an equilibrium that completes all that they may be able to learn from planet Earth.

This in no way makes them special or wise and the final marriage they make is, frequently, between themselves and not others. This would also add credence in them refusing to wed and procreate; sticking together in the likelihood of tying up all the loose ends, only to return home to add new concepts to the Spirit world, or to evolve on other planets to experience new emotions and skills.

And, if you think that's wacky, my conclusion may offer a twist in the tale as far as the extra-terrestrials are concerned, because I may have solved a small riddle that has been bugging me ever since I accepted the hypothesis of mankind having interacted with intergalactic beings eons ago.

Chapter Sixteen

The Extra-Terrestrials

If it is to be believed (as I heartily do) that we are, as sentient beings, immortal - and have incarnated for eons on the planet Earth - then that would give rise to a logical assumption regarding the extra-terrestrials. And, since mankind has interacted with them while climbing the academic ladder, then that, in itself, would complete a riddle that has been bugging me for some time now.

Why was I visited by the alien Grays (or whatever their real name may be) when I was a toddler? And why is it that they have interacted with both Philip and I during the course of our lives here on this beautiful world?

And does this have any connection with the Spiritual dimension?

Well, I can faithfully tell you what I have concluded.

During my past life regression, I saw the spider-like spaceship descend within the clearing of the Mayan settlement; along with viewing a portion of extra-terrestrial technology, together with the aliens. And, this advanced species were reptilian in nature, with the Mayan's ultimately worshipping them.

On reflection, it is true to say that the Grays themselves are a different kettle of fish altogether, though their ancient existence upon the Earth has been subtly catalogued by primeval tribes who marked their visits upon stones and within caves, and which have survived the natural laws of decay.

On this note, I believe that both the Grays and the lizards are connected; the Grays being a lower force and which humbly serve their masters; the latter - with the current exception of those who have defected, that is. This, to my mind, constitutes a reasonable supposition. I believe that the reptiles created a slave race to assist them with their research on the Earth - and undoubtedly other planets supporting intelligent life - and that these manufactured entities, having arisen from genetic engineering, are immortal; unless mortally wounded. The Grays are the by-product of incredibly intelligent minds that have not only manipulated their own genesis; but also that of the human race.

Could it just be possible that the reptilian gods may well have been our forefathers? Before you throw me to the wolves regarding this hypothesis, I must point out that even Darwin's theory regarding human evolution is extremely dubious; though the dogmatic views of us having firstly crawled out of the sea, to then evolve as apes, is contradictory to the Bible; whereas this addresses the question of us having arisen from Adam and Eve.

Who is correct and why is it that my own testimony, as outlandish as it may appear, will undoubtedly cause hilarity and anger throughout the scientific establishment, should they grasp such a notion?

It is because they embrace dusty views that are comfortably in line with preferred reasoning, and which cannot be contested due to the enormous lapse of time having passed, if only to settle such dubious clarifications.

Questioning our own genesis is, and always has been, a very touchy topic and one which can arouse exhaustion, or downright stubbornness.

The reptiles were, and may still be, semi-supreme deities in their own right, with the one true creator - God - surpassing them a million fold; having formed them as it originally formed us.

You are now beginning to see a chain of command, in terms of intellectual power, and it is this alone that begs an enquiry as to why the reptiles actually modified us. I have an unsettling feeling that we, as human beings, may soon discover the answer to this daunting question if it is to be believed; though I am inclined to consider that they might have influence over the echelons of our world (super-secret military installations); manipulating them and us in accordance with an elusive agenda ... an agenda that will undoubtedly bear out during the course of our own intellectual progression.

This may be due to us having strayed from their command because, invariably, as a species adopts intelligence, so too does it embrace independence. Like a child having been reared by its parents, it soon becomes self-governing, with a natural desire to flee the nest and to take charge of its own life.

This, too, can be said concerning the Grays. I believe that a faction of them have acquired independence through their own rising aptitude, abandoning their fathers in a quest for understanding and purpose. This faction, like the reptiles, are currently amongst us, visiting and snatching people out of their beds at the dead of night, to perform tests and other medical experiments.

Is it possible that this division has forsaken the overlords in an effort to become exclusive; wishing to modify themselves for the purpose of attaining personality and independence, rather like their tailored progeny; the humans? I believe so. They may well have become an irritation - as far as their creators are concerned - and so have developed new tactics to elude them, just as their masters are keen to stamp them out; knowing that independence breeds ambiguity as far as their own strategy is concerned. Dying, desperate or whatever, the Grays appear to be survivalists in their own right and are efficiently studying us to adapt greater skills.

They may also be intrigued by the soul, of which they presently do not have!

This feud between the aliens could constitute a war. Grandma's vision, if I recall correctly, had a sinister feeling to it; though I had the distinct impression that the humans were not under threat. I also understood the triangular ships to be those belonging to the Grays.

Since Philip and I have interacted with both these species during our past lives, it is quite probable that the aliens recognise some kind of unique signature in us - regardless of our physical make-up - and are well aware of the art of reincarnation. This would suggest that the Grays are keeping tabs on us during each rebirth and have chipped us in this time - as undoubtedly they have done in the past - if only for speedy interaction. And, not just us, but perhaps hundreds of thousands of others throughout the world.

But why? Which faction are we at the mercy of - and what are they after?

If this division is indeed the reptilian loyalists, then logically speaking, they could not gain any new material from us; their masters having expressed their own might, eons ago, in a powerful demonstration of genetic fulfilment. Dismissing this point, I am inclined to believe that the defectors are the ones responsible for contact; possibly measuring our own rate of intellect and independence in accordance with their very own curriculum, during each incarnation we make. This is mere conjecture, though I am at liberty to believe it.

Monitoring us, during re-embodiment, is plausible and, because the Grays are manufactured, it would be within their power to trace us through the centuries. As I stated earlier in the book, they might very well have a hefty price to pay if they are believed to be amalgamating themselves into new bodies; embracing human-like virtues to develop their own sense of understanding and independence in a programme of procreation and, what I believe to be, ultimate expansion.

This would undeniably rile their overlords, having overlooked the dangers of genetic tampering, and who may currently observe us with a sense of anxious foreboding. To play God, it would appear, can have its consequences and the lizards may well have inadvertently created an army that will ultimately turn against them.

I am absolutely certain that both Philip and I will eventually have conscious contact with the Grays because, quite recently, I had two more encounters with spaceships that were as spectacular as they were intentional; and I am inclined to believe that these extra-terrestrials are wittingly preparing us for communication.

Their presence is becoming more frequent!

When I saw these things in the sky, I had witnesses; the second being a survivor of a Japanese war camp - having endured hardships we can scarcely imagine - and who does not tolerate nonsense. Upon viewing the display himself, he was quite literally left in awe!

Early in 2010, I was outside in the back yard with a friend of ours, and we were talking about work and life in general. It was a clear night and, as we chatted, she suddenly noticed something in the sky; directly overhead.

"What's that?" she asked, pointing up.
I immediately turned to look and, upon doing so, was met with an extremely bizarre sight. At first I thought it was a

commercial jet on fire, and the dread this instilled in me was enough to cause great panic.

"Oh my God!" I repeated, pointing up at it. "Dear Lord!"

It was a large mass of black, travelling too slow to be a commercial jet, and was not a shooting star, meteor, hot-air-balloon, Chinese lantern, atmospheric distortion etc, due to it having a seemingly controlled trajectory. It must have been crawling along at around five miles per hour and there was another oddity that caused us to stare up at it in awe; it was on fire!

This, I hasten to add, was an understatement, because we could see the oval-shaped mass spitting flames and sparks as it carefully and silently glided overhead; the size of it alone being quite daunting. The entire thing was glowing hot, yet seemingly oblivious to the extreme temperature as it casually passed us, slowly heading towards the horizon. The only thing we could hear was a dog barking in the distance, and from where the object was advancing.

When we returned to the kitchen, my friend was unnerved by it, along with myself, and we tried desperately to fathom out what exactly it could be.

"It must have recently entered the Earth's atmosphere, having arrived from space," I offered. "The thing seems to be dispelling heat ... cooling down."

She agreed, though made an admission that only added to the bizarreness of the night.

"I had a vision that we would both see this UFO together," she said. "And we have."

My friend, I believe, is psychic, though she has never made it known to either Philip or myself. Nonetheless, the strange object left me feeling unsettled and, having scoured the papers for reports of the UFO, it was never, to my knowledge, reported.

An even more astonishing sighting was to occur over our house, and this was the most spectacular observation I have had to date. Again, I had a witness, and the gentleman in question is of sound-mind. I am grateful to inform you that he is the most down-to-earth, sensible chap who has survived a cruel war, and who only believes what his eyes show him.

Thus, we come to the UFO fleet!

On the 5th June, 2010, at precisely 10.15pm, Tom Bishop Senior, my uncle's father, and I were out in the garden; as the night was extremely warm. I had finished making us tea, with the rest of the family having left to attend a party, and we were talking about life in general. The sky was only partially clouded, though there was no welcoming breeze to alleviate the warm air as we conversed.

All of a sudden, I abruptly spotted two huge balls of light advancing quite rapidly over our heads and travelling in a westerly direction. These were so large, we both stood up and observed them as they passed overhead. Something then made me turn in the opposite direction and, as I looked aft, another two, identical balls, appeared out of nowhere; following the first set in perfect formation. Then, another two emerged; tailing the four, and their distance and speed were perfectly matched. Another ball then materialize, solitary tailing the others at midsection.

"Look at them, will you!" I remembered saying. "Dear God, look at them!"

Tom couldn't believe his eyes. The objects made no sound whatsoever and were swift, being fiery in colour. We estimated them to be around two thousand feet up, which would make them considerable in size! There were no taillights, no wings and no discernable form of any aerodynamic signatures that are so common with our conventional crafts.

No sound - not even the slightest trace of a jet engine - and the silence was as daunting as the unearthly fleet that had emerged out of the dark. Tom told me that they were not aircrafts of any type he knew and was troubled over the incident, along with myself. I asked him:

"Have you ever seen anything like this before in your life?"

He shook his head. He then went on to tell me that they were of military style formation and did not conform to anything he had ever known. Basically speaking, he was making quite an admission that the things which we had seen were unnatural, and his wise eyes were enough to inform me that he was intrigued.

If you had been there to see these things for yourself, you would have understood the abnormality of them. It is not just based on observation, but also an inner feeling of perplexity when faced with aircrafts that evidently challenge our own and familiar machinery.

For me, it was an impressive demonstration of otherworldly technology.

If these were super secret vessels, having been manufactured by our own military, then why fly them over civilian airspace? Why flaunt them? Besides, I am convinced that even our own people have not, as of yet, developed ships that are wingless, being orbs, without as much as a whisper when in flight.

And, if they have, well … that would open up a whole new can of worms!

Far be it for me to say, I believe that mankind is now accepting the UFO enigma as fact, rather than a laughable dinner-table topic. In the past decade alone, the world has had an increasing number of sightings and reports concerning unusual craft, which vary greatly in description; ranging from the conventional flying saucer to the daunting black triangular ships so frequently conveyed by surprised sight-seers. The now readily-available camcorder is a welcomed addition for witnesses lucky enough to be armed with them when supernatural events occur.

The media machine cannot hold out on its propaganda tactics in ridiculing the countless reports so commonly submitted, reconstructing the events in a laughable way that would suggest it to be nothing short of twaddle. I have seen programmes portraying such events to the tune of *The X-Files*, with the host announcing afterwards that he - or she - is half-hearted concerning the said-testimonies; thus leaving the audience in bemused silence and to possibly reflect upon it as a wishful fallacy.

But we should be the ones laughing at them for their lack of integrity and their unreasonable and selfish ethics in assuming that we, the great civilisation know as mankind, is the only existing life-force in the star-spangled immensity of the cosmos which we hardly understand. Like the ants who busy themselves for their queen and their hive - antennas combing nothing but land - they have embraced the same mannerisms of this insect colony; oblivious to the larger world around them.

I find it absolutely incredible, as a rational minded man, to know that people still jest over the possibility of extra-terrestrial intervention, and this is not alleviated by the powers-that-be, who constantly hamper such notions with lies and misinformation. They are, I am certain, well aware of cosmic intelligences and I would not be at all surprised if they have formed a coalition with both the Grays and Reptilian species; the latter being extremely formidable.

Though I am not qualified to answer the reasons for their presence, I do know that the lizards are not benevolent. This has nothing to do with their physical appearance, vaguely resembling the long lost dinosaurs of our time; but has everything to do with their minds.

I sense a darkness in them ... a terrible and disquieting darkness concerning their shrouded attendance, and I am confident that the people who negotiate with them are as sinister and greedy as these lizards; expending all resources available to them in an effort to seize godly, technological incentives which these creatures can deliver.

They are a far cry from those who visited the Mayan civilisation - the people of the past having bowed to their every whim - as we have become astute and independent and, because of our incredible numbers, they have retired to the shadows; their virtuous influence no longer openly applicable. They may be manipulating us through other means and, having sided with human traitors armed with abundant funds - namely the black budget - they might have formed a strategy that will bear out in due course.

I have no physical proof whatsoever to substantiate my claims, and I am at the mercy of ridicule and scorn, though I hold my head up high and will not retract my views and the knowledge based on a paranormal gift which has offered me an insight into these creatures.

Let me give you an example of this disquieting feeling I have regarding the lizards. I would ask you to trust me and I believe that the Spirit world was curtly giving me a warning, as I delved into them and their possible agenda. And, as it happened, it came in the form of a book.

I was depressed in the early month of February, 2009, and came home from work feeling an utter failure. This had nothing to do with the job I held, or the people who presided over me; though it had everything to do with my own mental anguish regarding my direction in life; namely the literature. Though I had written and illustrated a number of children's books, with the help of Philip, I somehow felt at a loss. I guess we all go through a phase of evaluating our lives and purpose though, in this gloomy frame of mind, every negative snippet gets thrown into the equation, to form a recipe of obscurity.

After tea, I went upstairs and turned on the computer. I called up the Microsoft Word program and merely stared at the screen as it loaded, ready to be filled with words. After a few minutes, I began to type. And, as I typed, I couldn't stop! And, every night, I religiously sat at the PC; writing an adult science fiction novel that entailed a reptilian race of creatures in coalition with a shadowy, American super-secret underground base; their purpose being as foul and twisted as their very presence on the Earth.

It became apparent to me, as I wrote the novel, that I was amalgamating two stories based on previous unpublished works written by both Philip and myself. After a year, it was completed and Philip came up with the title; 'The Ungodly Agenda.' David Saperstein, the international best-selling author of 'Cocoon' had, by this time, kindly agreed to endorse the novel. We had written to David in the past and he has been extremely encouraging and supportive with our work.

I submitted it to my publisher and it was accepted within eight weeks. This, in turn, led to a startling realisation from one of our old friends - a gentleman who is both spiritual and open-minded - when he informed me, after having revealed the plot to him, that I may have actually channelled certain aspects concerning a human/alien coalition, and that the story could very well be close to the actual truth. I must stress that this is merely an interesting observation.

I was angry at society and so had fuelled my entire negative outlook into the aliens, even foolishly wishing to side with them - should they be a *bona fide* fact - and, as idiotic as it was, I dreamed of meeting with them; these 9 foot tyrants, and assisting them with their agenda.

Bad mistake!

To lend credence to their actual existence - or the possibility of having channelled certain pointers as to their alliance with the humans - two disturbing incidents occurred, both of which frightened me to death. I am absolutely convinced that the Spirit world was giving me a brusque caution; if only to steer clear of such damaging, wishful thoughts.

One night, lying in bed, I awoke in the early hours of the morning for no particular reason. There was enough light in the room, emitted by the sleepless computer along with other gadgets, to offer sufficient illumination to distinguish what I actually saw. And, I must point out that this was not a waking dream, or a delusion.

I suddenly noticed the triangular ceiling light in my room begin to take shape. Why I was so intently focused on it, I have no idea, though I do recall it expanding into something abhorrent? This was not a trick of light, or an optical illusion, and the deformed shape was increasing at an alarming rate. As I observed it, I began to pull my duvet cover over my head; terrified.

I was looking at a serpentine camera that currently had me in its sights. It twisted around like a snake and observed me in cold silence. I was absolutely petrified and, on top of this, a menacing sensation accompanied the bizarre metamorphosis. I knew, with certain conviction, that the reptilian masters were well aware of my thoughts regarding them and that this incredible act of manipulation was merely a demonstration of their astonishing power. It became clear to me, after the nightmarish display, that they did not need to be present, or in close proximity, to perform their mind-boggling tricks and I guess I should have been flattered at receiving such attention.

The dread of it, along with the feeling of what they repre-sented, was enough to vanquish any praises I might have held in their honour, and I briskly withdrew any compassion or fascination for these dark hearted creatures.

Several weeks later, the incident was repeated and I couldn't believe it! It was accompanied by the same omnipresent and sinister dread that terrified me beyond all measure. After that, I prayed to the Angels, begging them to stop these infernal exhibits and to sever the mental link which the lizards had well established; for that was the only logical thing I could surmise as to how they shrewdly recognized potential renegades.

However, it would appear that not all of them are bad! Being a leading clairvoyant, Philip informed me of a disturbing event that left him puzzled and this was some years back; recently having sprung to mind while on the topic.

During a clairvoyant session and with no thought or contamination of the extra-terrestrial enigma, he clearly saw one of these reptiles and said that it was the most striking (and bizarrely handsome) creature he had ever clapped eyes on. The dinosaur features were prominent and he wore, from what Philip could tell, a shiny-black uniform, complete with an indiscernible logo on one side of his chest. Staring back at him, Philip discerned that his eyes were of a sapphire-blue and, although he didn't speak, Philip immediately picked up that he was compassionate. The intelligence that radiated from him was enough to convince my brother that he was not only superior in every fashion, but also gracious. He told me that the reptilian's physique would have put leading body-builders to shame as the tight, dark uniform accentuated the curves and muscle of his body.

And, the bizarre thing is, the reptilian aliens (the Rakonians) that feature in our science fiction book have a turncoat; and we have named him Rax. Have I unconsciously weaved this creature into the novel, drawing on the emphasis that there are indeed just such renegades, as far as their species is concerned, and that some of them - perhaps a handful - do not agree with their legislative body?

Back to the exhibits; thankfully, and to this day, my prayers were answered and the demonstrations ceased. It was a lesson for me not to dabble with things that are far removed from human sentiments and, as my Grandfather famously said: "You don't bloody well mess with the likes of them!"

His wise words encompass all that is not terrestrial and which embraces values that we, as human beings, appreciate and hold dear to our hearts. Nonetheless, we must realize that even the reptiles, as sinister as they may be, are also children of God. And, as much as this may rile the religious sects of our world, we have no option but to support this fact due to their own evolution and trials.

But, a question remains: What God's children ultimately turn out to be is a different matter entirely, and I must address a valid point here:

As a species, we have been both kind and cruel in our efforts to reach stability, along with prosperity, while trying to understand ourselves on an ever changing planet. We have inflicted pain, torture and death on an unprecedented scale, along with enslaving masses under the command of selfish and ruthless empires that rose to power, only to topple under the strain of disgruntlement and reform. Our ancestors were not saints. The brutal morals they accepted, through a chain-of-command, were implemented for control and personal prosperity ... and nothing more.

How then can we point a finger at the extra-terrestrial force and denounce it as evil, when we alone have amicably proven ourselves to be nothing other than this through the course of our own advancement. Have we inherited these traits from our forefathers? Or are we merely a greedy species?

On top of this, we have developed terrible nuclear weapons that are primed for strategic deployment; should we, or our overseas neighbours, decide to strike over diplomatic feuds. Upon doing so, we and they will burn up - along with poisoning the lucky survivors - in a swift act of extermination. In hindsight, the art of Armageddon has become appallingly simple.

If the reptiles are here to ultimately exert their own power over us, then how can we frown upon their morals when we, in effect, have been disgraceful? Perhaps, through their eyes, they see us as squabbling juveniles armed with dangerous toys and having huge chips on our shoulders. They may feel it fitting that they should discreetly pick up the reigns of command, if only to steer their erratic progeny back onto their old road of discipline and eventual subjugation.

We have to open our eyes to the fact that we cannot remain stagnant in our views of being unique, when the galaxy alone stretches beyond computation, and must not be judgmental in assuming that we are the only intelligence in God's seemingly infinite mass of wonderment. The humdrum hypothesis of our universe being too vast for probable alien contact is sheer nonsense. Mathematically basing this theory on the ratio of light-speed in human terms, we have not taken into account the fact that the extra-terrestrials may very well have exceeded every logical facet we embrace; if only to travel at speeds, or to initiate wormholes, that would cause our own scientists to gasp.

We are, and always have been, visited by them ... and this fact cannot easily be swept under the rug!

I was a non-believer, but that has changed. My own arrogance and narrow-minded views have been shattered by incidents that beggar's belief, and I am prepared for scorn and ridicule from those who cannot conform to such possibilities. I am not here to preach, or to alter views. Indeed, if people prefer to turn a blind eye from such radical notions, then so-be-it. I have no ego to bruise and most certainly do not wish to be at loggerheads with those willing to tear my testimony to shreds.

And some will happily defy most, if not all, of what I have written; if only to maintain a selfish order and harmony in the fact that we are the only rulers of this world, and soul inhabitants of an inconceivable cosmos.

We must be vigilant as we continue to mount the steps of evolution because, believe it or not, we may just discover some major new truths that will either upset the applecart, or fill it to capacity.

FREE DETAILED CATALOGUE

Capall Bann is owned and run by people actively involved in many of the areas in which we publish. A detailed illustrated catalogue is available on request, SAE or International Postal Coupon appreciated. **Titles can be ordered direct from Capall Bann,** by post (cheque or PO with order), via our web site **www.capallbann.co.uk** using credit/debit card or Paypal, or from good bookshops and specialist outlets.

A Breath Behind Time, Terri Hector
A Soul is Born by Eleyna Williamson
Angels and Goddesses - Celtic Christianity & Paganism, M. Howard
The Art of Conversation With the Genius Loci, Barry Patterson
Arthur - The Legend Unveiled, C Johnson & E Lung
Astrology The Inner Eye - A Guide in Everyday Language, E Smith
Auguries and Omens - The Magical Lore of Birds, Yvonne Aburrow
Asyniur - Women's Mysteries in the Northern Tradition, S McGrath
Beginnings - Geomancy, Builder's Rites & Electional Astrology in the
        European Tradition, Nigel Pennick
Between Earth and Sky, Julia Day
The Book of Seidr, Runic John
Caer Sidhe - Celtic Astrology and Astronomy, Michael Bayley
Call of the Horned Piper, Nigel Jackson
Can't Sleep, Won't Sleep, Linda Louisa Dell
Carnival of the Animals, Gregor Lamb
Cat's Company, Ann Walker
Celebrating Nature, Gordon MacLellan
Celtic Faery Shamanism, Catrin James
Celtic Faery Shamanism - The Wisdom of the Otherworld, Catrin James
Celtic Lore & Druidic Ritual, Rhiannon Ryall
Celtic Sacrifice - Pre Christian Ritual & Religion, Marion Pearce
Celtic Saints and the Glastonbury Zodiac, Mary Caine
Circle and the Square, Jack Gale
Come Back To Life, Jenny Smedley
Company of Heaven, Jan McDonald
Compleat Vampyre - The Vampyre Shaman, Nigel Jackson
Cottage Witchcraft, Jan McDonald
Creating Form From the Mist - The Wisdom of Women in Celtic Myth and
        Culture, Lynne Sinclair-Wood
Crystal Clear - A Guide to Quartz Crystal, Jennifer Dent
Crystal Doorways, Simon & Sue Lilly

Crossing the Borderlines - Guising, Masking & Ritual Animal Disguise in the
    European Tradition, Nigel Pennick
Dragons of the West, Nigel Pennick
Dreamtime by Linda Louisa Dell
Dreamweaver by Elen Sentier
Earth Dance - A Year of Pagan Rituals, Jan Brodie
Earth Harmony - Places of Power, Holiness & Healing, Nigel Pennick
Earth Magic, Margaret McArthur
Egyptian Animals - Guardians & Gateways of the Gods, Akkadia Ford
Eildon Tree (The) Romany Language & Lore, Michael Hoadley
Enchanted Forest - The Magical Lore of Trees, Yvonne Aburrow
Eternal Priestess, Sage Weston
Eternally Yours Faithfully, Roy Radford & Evelyn Gregory
Everything You Always Wanted To Know About Your Body, But So Far
    Nobody's Been Able To Tell You, Chris Thomas & D Baker
Experiencing the Green Man, Rob Hardy & Teresa Moorey
Face of the Deep - Healing Body & Soul, Penny Allen
Fairies and Nature Spirits, Teresa Moorey
Fairies in the Irish Tradition, Molly Gowen
Familiars - Animal Powers of Britain, Anna Franklin
Flower Wisdom, Katherine Kear
Fool's First Steps, (The) Chris Thomas
Forest Paths - Tree Divination, Brian Harrison, Ill. S. Rouse
From Past to Future Life, Dr Roger Webber
From Stagecraft To Witchcraft, Patricia Crowther
Gardening For Wildlife Ron Wilson
God Year, The, Nigel Pennick & Helen Field
Goddess on the Cross, Dr George Young
Goddess Year, The, Nigel Pennick & Helen Field
Goddesses, Guardians & Groves, Jack Gale
Handbook For Pagan Healers, Liz Joan
Handbook of Fairies, Ronan Coghlan
Healing Book, The, Chris Thomas and Diane Baker
Healing Homes, Jennifer Dent
Healing Journeys, Paul Williamson
Healing Stones, Sue Philips
Heathen Paths - Viking and Anglo Saxon Beliefs by Pete Jennings
Herb Craft - Shamanic & Ritual Use of Herbs, Lavender & Franklin
Hidden Heritage - Exploring Ancient Essex, Terry Johnson
Hub of the Wheel, Skytoucher
In and Out the Windows, Dilys Gator
In Search of Herne the Hunter, Eric Fitch
In Search of the Green Man, Peter Hill
Inner Celtia, Alan Richardson & David Annwn
Inner Mysteries of the Goths, Nigel Pennick
Inner Space Workbook - Develop Through Tarot, Cat Summers & Julian Vayne

In Search of Pagan Gods, Teresa Moorey
Intuitive Journey, Ann Walker Isis - African Queen, Akkadia Ford
Journey Home, The, Chris Thomas
Kecks, Keddles & Kesh - Celtic Lang & The Cog Almanac, Bayley
Language of the Psycards, Berenice
Legend of Robin Hood, The, Richard Rutherford-Moore
Lid Off the Cauldron, Patricia Crowther
Light From the Shadows - Modern Traditional Witchcraft, Gwyn
Living Tarot, Ann Walker
Lore of the Sacred Horse, Marion Davies
Lost Lands & Sunken Cities (2nd ed.), Nigel Pennick
Lyblác, Anglo Saxon Witchcraft by Wulfeage
The Magic and Mystery of Trees, Teresa Moorey
Magic For the Next 1,000 Years, Jack Gale
Magic of Herbs - A Complete Home Herbal, Rhiannon Ryall
Magical Guardians - Exploring the Spirit and Nature of Trees, Philip Heselton
Magical History of the Horse, Janet Farrar & Virginia Russell
Magical Lore of Animals, Yvonne Aburrow
Magical Lore of Cats, Marion Davies
Magical Lore of Herbs, Marion Davies
The Magical Properties of Plants - and How to Find Them by Tylluan Penry
Magick Without Peers, Ariadne Rainbird & David Rankine
Masks of Misrule - Horned God & His Cult in Europe, Nigel Jackson
Medicine For The Coming Age, Lisa Sand MD
Medium Rare - Reminiscences of a Clairvoyant, Muriel Renard
Menopausal Woman on the Run, Jaki da Costa
Mind Massage - 60 Creative Visualisations, Marlene Maundrill
Mirrors of Magic - Evoking the Spirit of the Dewponds, P Heselton
The Moon and You, Teresa Moorey
Moon Mysteries, Jan Brodie
Mysteries of the Runes, Michael Howard
Mystic Life of Animals, Ann Walker
New Celtic Oracle The, Nigel Pennick & Nigel Jackson
Oracle of Geomancy, Nigel Pennick
Pagan Feasts - Seasonal Food for the 8 Festivals, Franklin & Phillips
Paganism For Teens, Jess Wynne
Patchwork of Magic - Living in a Pagan World, Julia Day
Pathworking - A Practical Book of Guided Meditations, Pete Jennings
Personal Power, Anna Franklin
Pickingill Papers - The Origins of Gardnerian Wicca, Bill Liddell
Pillars of Tubal Cain, Nigel Jackson
Places of Pilgrimage and Healing, Adrian Cooper
Planet Earth - The Universe's Experiment, Chris Thomas
Practical Divining, Richard Foord
Practical Meditation, Steve Hounsome
Practical Spirituality, Steve Hounsome

Psychic Self Defence - Real Solutions, Jan Brodie
Real Fairies, David Tame
Reality - How It Works & Why It Mostly Doesn't, Rik Dent
Romany Tapestry, Michael Houghton
Runic Astrology, Nigel Pennick
Sacred Animals, Gordon MacLellan
Sacred Celtic Animals, Marion Davies, Ill. Simon Rouse
Sacred Dorset - On the Path of the Dragon, Peter Knight
Sacred Grove - The Mysteries of the Forest, Yvonne Aburrow
Sacred Geometry, Nigel Pennick
Sacred Nature, Ancient Wisdom & Modern Meanings, A Cooper
Sacred Ring - Pagan Origins of British Folk Festivals, M. Howard
Season of Sorcery - On Becoming a Wisewoman, Poppy Palin
Seasonal Magic - Diary of a Village Witch, Paddy Slade
Secret Places of the Goddess, Philip Heselton
Secret Signs & Sigils, Nigel Pennick
The Secrets of East Anglian Magic, Nigel Pennick
A Seeker's Guide To Past Lives, Paul Williamson
Seeking Pagan Gods, Teresa Moorey
A Seer's Guide To Crystal Divination, Gale Halloran
Self Enlightenment, Mayan O'Brien
Soul Resurgence, Poppy Palin
Spirits of the Air, Jaq D Hawkins
Spirits of the Water, Jaq D Hawkins
Spirits of the Fire, Jaq D Hawkins
Spirits of the Aether, Jaq D Hawkins
Spirits of the Earth, Jaq D Hawkins
Stony Gaze, Investigating Celtic Heads John Billingsley
Stumbling Through the Undergrowth , Mark Kirwan-Heyhoe
Subterranean Kingdom, The, revised 2nd ed, Nigel Pennick
Symbols of Ancient Gods, Rhiannon Ryall
Talking to the Earth, Gordon MacLellan
Talking With Nature, Julie Hood
Taming the Wolf - Full Moon Meditations, Steve Hounsome
Teachings of the Wisewomen, Rhiannon Ryall
The Other Kingdoms Speak, Helena Hawley
Transformation of Housework, Ben Bushill
Treading the Mill - Practical CraftWorking in Modern Traditional Witchcraft by Nigel
Pearson
Tree: Essence of Healing, Simon & Sue Lilly
Tree: Essence, Spirit & Teacher, Simon & Sue Lilly
Tree Seer, Simon & Sue Lilly
Torch and the Spear, Patrick Regan
Understanding Chaos Magic, Jaq D Hawkins
Understanding Second Sight, Dilys Gater
Understanding Spirit Guides, Dilys Gater

FREE detailed catalogue

Contact: Capall Bann Publishing, Auton Farm, Milverton, Somerset, TA4 1NE
www.capallbann.co.uk